LIVING WITH *SCHIZOPHRENIA*

LIVING WITH *SCHIZOPHRENIA*

Alexander P. Hyde, M.D.

CONTEMPORARY
BOOKS, INC.
CHICAGO

Library of Congress Cataloging in Publication Data

Hyde, Alexander, 1925–
Living with schizophrenia.

Includes index.
1. Schizophrenia. 2. Schizophrencs—Home care.
Schizophrenics—Rehabilitation. I. Title.
[DNLM: 1. Schizophrenia—Popular works.
WM203 H993L]
RC514.H92 1980 616.89'82 79-50980
ISBN 0-8092-5665-7 ISBN 0-8092-5262-7 pbk

Published by Contemporary Books, Inc.
180 North Michigan Avenue, Chicago, Illinois 60601
Manufactured in the United States of America
International Standard Book Number: 0-8092-5262-7

Published simultaneously in Canada by Beaverbooks, Ltd.
195 Allstate Parkway, Valleywood Business Park
Markham, Ontario L3R 4T8 Canada

To my nifty wife Mary

Contents

Introduction

This book was written because no publications were available that presented a simple explanation of the modern treatment of schizophrenia at home. Most of the patients I see in my office have no idea of how to manage the many problems that arise during and after the acute illness. In addition, if the truth be known, very few counselors and psychiatrists are either knowledgeable or interested in rehabilitation of schizophrenics.

My interest in the field arose from having a lengthy, serious illness (not schizophrenia) while I was a medical student and young doctor. This experience left me with an enduring wish to spare others the agonies I suffered. Looking back, if I had had a clear idea of how to manage my recovery I might have saved months—even a year or two—of intense suffering and disability.

With my complete recovery came an exciting variety of professional activities. I became a private psychotherapist, a geriatric psychiatrist, the director of a day-care center, the director of a large clinic at Boston City Hospital, medical director of a halfway house, a mission hospital psychiatrist, a writer and researcher, and in later years a medical psychiatrist in private practice. These activities resulted in a fortuitous blend of experience in rehabilitation, which resulted in the development of practical guidelines for the treatment of schizophrenia. It became clear that if patients and families followed these guidelines carefully, in most instances they could raise the level of recovery of the schizophrenic—above, in fact, anything they and their families thought possible, and very often to the point of functional cure.

Because most families and patients are so upset during the duration of the acute illness, this book was written as simply as possible. We felt the format of answering the questions most often asked by patients and families in the office would be best.

If this book makes any single point, I hope it is to stress the importance of practicing simple, good daily health habits in the rehabilitiation of every disorder such as schizophrenia. Without the development of such a basic health style, the effectiveness of other treatments is, at best, hit or miss.

Hopefully the book also makes clear how important the toxic elements (certain drugs, foods, and unpleasant living conditions) are in sabotaging an otherwise effective rehabilitation program.

The other main message of the book is to teach meticulous observance of the dos and don'ts because good execution, as with an athletic team, often makes the difference between mediocre and truly amazing recoveries.

One other matter prompted the writing of this book and that is that it is becoming clear to those of us who work with schizophrenia that untreated, frequently relapsing schizophrenics often get worse as time goes on. Happily, it also seems clear that this typically progressive deterioration can be arrested by preventing relapses—a compelling motive for the patient and family to learn to manage the disorder!

1

Schizophrenia—fact and myth

What is schizophrenia?

"Schizophrenia" is more than a single disorder; the term actually encompasses several disorders, each of which is distinct from the others in some way. Like the childhood diseases—mumps, German measles, whooping cough, and measles—the various types of schizophrenia differ from each other in some ways but are similar in others. All the schizophrenias are brain disorders—physical, metabolic disturbances of the brain. In other words, each type affects the brain functions of perception, thinking, emotion, and coordination of movement.

During the past fifteen years, we have learned more about the nature of schizophrenia. Namely, the nerve impulses of the schizophrenic pass between the brain cells in an abnormal manner. Imagine that the brain is a computer with faulty connections between elements, so that too many impulses (multiple short circuits of some nature) get through. The whole brain mechanism then becomes flooded with impulses, with the cells in the affected areas of the brain becoming overactive and easily stimulated. The result is that the entire system is overwhelmed.

The specific areas that are apparently involved in schizophrenic disorders lie deep within the brain and affect the way emotions, thoughts, feelings, and perceptions operate together. A normal person who sees a strawberry sundae may think about how delicious it looks and begin to drool. But the same strawberries might appear to a schizophrenic as poisoned berries that must be avoided at all costs. The schizophrenic's perceptions, thinking, and emotions are not working normally; the connections are not right. When the schizophrenic process is active, the afflicted person cannot count on the accuracy of messages received by the brain. The patient lives in a state of constant uncertainty, like a dream, in which people, objects, places, and thoughts are always changing. Important faculties, feelings, and impulses controlled by the brain—concentration, interest, hope, pleasure, love, initiative, and ambition, for example—are usually affected, making the schizophrenic's conscious life a never-ending internal chaos.

Doesn't schizophrenia mean "split personality"?

According to *Webster's*, "schizo" comes from the Greek verb meaning "to split." "Phrenia," also derived from a Greek root, means "mind." The "split" in schizophrenia refers to the altered state of mind that controls the schizophrenic—the change from one who is actively sick to one who is well. Schizophrenia does not imply "split personality," which is a separate disorder and is not usually considered a form of schizophrenia. However, schizophrenics occasionally do come to believe they are very important figures, such as Jesus or a famous queen. But these delusions are symptoms that fade and are replaced by normal thinking and reality as the brain begins to function better with treatment. After their condition improves, schizophrenics describe this change as a gradual awakening from a dream—the dream and awake states as two separate and distinct mental states.

Is schizophrenia caused by childhood problems and emotional disturbances?

No. The basic cause is an organic, structural, chemical disorder of the brain cells. Schizophrenia is a disorder of the brain in the same way that diabetes is a disorder of the pancreas. Like diabetics, whose condition worsens when they stray from the proper regimen, schizophrenics feel ill when their good health habits deteriorate. Inadequate sleep, poor eating habits, ingestion of coffee and alcohol, and lack of exercise cause the schizophrenic condition to worsen. Continued intense emotional stress also can overstimulate the schizophrenic, with adverse effects.

Research has shown no cause-and-effect relationship between an unhappy childhood and the onset of schizophrenia. In fact, relatively few schizophrenics seem to have had particularly unusual childhoods. In retrospect, the mothers of many recovered schizophrenics report that the children did show early signs of schizophrenia, that they were somehow different from their brothers or sisters. Many of these people seemed overactive or more sensitive and vulnerable as young children, which often gave their mothers a tendency to overprotect them. But for the most part, the families reported that the children were normal and happy before the onset of schizophrenia. Some schizophrenics of course, experienced cruelty, alcoholism, and lack of love in the family during childhood, but these conditions probably aggravate, rather than cause, the schizophrenia.

Can parents cause the development of schizophrenia in their children?

No parent could possibly want a child to become mentally ill, nor is it possible to cause such disorders. Even today, nobody could tell parents how to cause schizophrenia. The myth that parents cause schizophrenia is unfounded. Heredity and a number of other physical factors, often aggravated by emotional stress, cause schizophrenia, not the environment created by parents for their children. The most that emotional stresses can do to the growing child is to worsen the schizophrenic disorder. In most cases, such influences are unavoidable and, regardless of the childhood atmosphere, the schizophrenia probably would come about sooner or later.

It is important to realize that even when emotional stress is not responsible for the development of a physical disorder, it can and does worsen the victim's condition. Arthritis, heart trouble, asthma and diabetes are all adversely affected by emotional strain, as is schizophrenia, but none of them is directly caused by emotional stress. It is reported that even broken legs heal more slowly when the patient is subjected to continued intense emotional stress.

At what age does schizophrenia come on?

Like diabetes, schizophrenia can come on at any time in one's life—from the age of two or three to the age of sixty-five. Most commonly, however, the disorder shows up during the late teens or early twenties. It affects men and women about equally, and spares no particular race or economic class. Childhood schizophrenia is rare, which is fortunate since it is difficult to treat and needs special professional attention. Schizophrenia may come on after marriage, too. This presents special problems, but the outlook for a well-treated married schizophrenic is usually excellent, because the best features of rehabilitation and health maintenance are available in this kind of family structure.

No one knows why a particular person comes down with any chronic illness at a certain age. Why a schizophrenic's symptoms first appear at age sixteen or forty, rather than at some other age, is also a mystery.

How can schizophrenics and their families manage the disorder?

Many things can be done to improve the condition of those with disorders like schizophrenia and diabetes. Schizophrenia, like diabetes, is never cured, but good treatment can often produce the *appearance* of a total cure. Current knowledge of the disorder includes a great deal of information about the symptoms, course, and other characteristics of schizophrenia, as well as its treatment.

The following chapters offer fundamental treatment for various types of schizophrenia, including guidelines for sleeping, eating, exercise, activity, work, and medication. They also clarify the attitude the patient should have toward the disorder and proper behavior of family members toward the schizophrenic during various stages of recovery. Factual information is given on the daily management of schizophrenia and the many problems involving stigma, reentering normal social life, automobile driving, sex, and even how to handle doctors! An important section of the book focuses on the hazards and benefits of the various medications commonly used in the treatment of schizophrenia.

Does having schizophrenia mean that one will end up in the back ward of a mental hospital or suffer insanity for the rest of his or her life?

No! Absolutely not. Schizophrenia is a very mild disorder in some people, moderate in others, and very severe in still others. Each type varies a great deal from one person to another. The outlook is very much an individual matter, but only a few people end up permanently in mental hospitals or nursing homes.

Until recently, little was known about effective rehabilitation of schizophrenia. To this day, truly superior care and treatment is not available everywhere. However, in recent years new medications, new knowledge about lifestyles and bodily rhythms, and new information on allergies and nutrition have been developed. Even under the current system of care and treatment, however, few patients stay in mental hospitals for any length of time.

Should schizophrenics and their families be completely informed about the diagnosis of the disorder?

This is a very important matter. When mental illness strikes a family member, the family is naturally upset; learning that the illness is schizophrenia rarely produces additional distress. Everyone—patient and family—knows that something dreadful is happening and wants the problem diagnosed and treated as quickly as possible. To them, hearing the word "schizophrenia," which is a disorder that usually can be treated effectively, *is normally a relief rather than a shock.* Naturally, a responsible physician will not name a disorder until he or she has fully studied the person and has made use of appropriate psychological and laboratory tests and X rays. But there is no reason for secrecy once a diagnosis is made.

Many families and patients have been frustrated by visits to a variety of treatment facilities, where a frank diagnosis has been cloaked in such terms as "depression" and "emotional disorder." Well-meaning doctors may believe that withholding the diagnosis of schizophrenia spares the patient and family from the stigma attached to the disorder. It is a fact that mental illnesses in our society have been looked down on and stigmatized. As a result, many doctors do not wish to upset the patients and their families with their diagnoses, even though they always appear officially on medical records. In addition, there has been a tendency in psychiatry during the past fifty years to blame the family for the schizophrenic's plight. Somehow, the family of the schizophrenic has been stereotyped as less intelligent and less capable of caring or less willing to care for the patient than, say, the families of patients with other disorders.

In some cases, professionals in health fields do not believe schizophrenia is a physical, medical disorder of the brain because so much can be done for schizophrenia through the nonmedical, corrective social types of treatment detailed in this book. They believe that naming such a disorder may cause the patient and family to expect a medical cure, which, of course, will not occur without the full involvement of the patient and family.

We believe the word *schizophrenia* itself must be used so that schizophrenics and families, like diabetics and their families, can intelligently and effectively manage the disorder. Schizophrenics and their families repeatedly emphasize that not knowing the diagnosis of the disorder makes them unable to cooperate in its treatment. The unknown is always much worse than the known. No one keeps the diagnosis of diabetes a secret to spare the feelings of the patient because the diabetic and family must learn how to care for it, read up on it, join the Diabetes Association, and keep abreast of advances in the treatment of diabetes. Psychologically, such ignorance makes the patient and family feel inferior to the doctor because they are less informed, less confident, and less responsible. Because the patient and family are responsible for ninety percent of the treatment in any long-term disorder, ignorance of the disorder's nature makes it difficult to take responsibility for it.

Schizophrenics who really wish to be well must become experts in the treatment of the disorder because they alone can truly care for themselves.

Today, with the improved outlook for schizophrenia victims, the diagnosis need not be disguised. Patients and families can and do learn to handle schizophrenia, just as they would handle any other long-term illness. Clearly, in the past, the problem has been that neither the patient nor the family knew what to do or how to do it. Once they learn the facts, there rarely is a problem with cooperation or attitude in the family.

Families of patients are often ingenious in solving their problems once they learn about the disorder and the principles of its treatment. A great portion of the practical information included in this book was gleaned from listening to and observing a great many patients and their families during successful recoveries.

Is the treatment of schizophrenia really effective?

Yes. Just ask any diabetic if *his* treatment works. Every diabetic knows how rundown, ill, and chronically "blah" he or she feels when not following the daily regime of proper diet, exercise, medications, sleep, and fun. When diabetics and schizophrenics take care of themselves by maintaining good physical condition and the correct weight, by following rules of good nutrition, and adapting the right pace in their lifestyles, their whole sense of well-being improves enormously to make them lively, full of fun and purpose.

Probably the greatest thing schizophrenic patients and their families learn is how astonishingly effective this super-healthy lifestyle is. Really dramatic changes do not usually become evident until two or three months of care have passed, but considerable improvement often occurs within ten days. Families and patients who have visited our office constantly say, "I never believed she would really get so well"; "Just think, a year ago Paul was in a back ward and now he's working nearly full time in a restaurant!"; "I thought I'd never get back to my electronic research lab again!"

These successful patients and families have taken two basic steps. One is to accept the disorder of schizophrenia for what it is. The second step is to make every possible effort to lessen the effects of the schizophrenia, exactly as the diabetic and family do. That is, like diabetics, schizophrenics can and do learn to take good care of their bodies, live sensibly, take few drugs (coffee, alcohol, marijuana), take their medications correctly, and eat properly. They benefit from the remarkable improvement that results from this care.

2

The three basic schizophrenic disorders

What are the various types of schizophrenia?

Today most authorities talk about three basic disorders: acute schizophrenia, process schizophrenia, and paranoid schizophrenia. *Acute schizophrenia* is characterized by explosive, stormy episodes that last for much shorter periods—up to a few weeks—than the other two types. This type is the easiest schizophrenia to treat.* *Process schizophrenia* is probably the most common type; it takes longer to develop and longer to improve than the acute type. *Paranoid schizophrenia* also follows a longer course at the start and may require a longer rehabilitation period. All three types are treated with similar basic antipsychotic medications and rehabilitative processes.

*also chronic undifferentiated schizophrenia

What does the term "paranoid" mean?

Paranoid means characterized by suspiciousness, delusions of persecution or grandeur, and distrust, according to *Webster's*. Paranoid people are extremely self-conscious, feeling that others are talking about them and plotting against them. In paranoid schizophrenia this pattern of thought and behavior is a major consistent feature. Paranoid schizophrenics have delusions—false, fixed beliefs—that they are being hunted, persecuted, or attacked. They may hallucinate, hearing voices and sounds of people and things not actually present, for example.

Paranoid schizophrenics are actually fearful, but they try to act cool and unaffected. They are always extra-alert and stay on guard even when with their closest loved ones. They trust no one, keeping a distance from everyone. Because paranoid schizophrenics feel they are the center of everyone's attention, they often develop the conviction that they control the vital secrets of the universe. This overwhelming feeling of self-importance may lead schizophrenics to become extremely religious, especially during the onset of the disorder. In some cases, paranoid schizophrenics suffer the delusion that they have become important figures from the past or present, as mentioned in Chapter 1.

What is process schizophrenia?

"Process" refers to the gradual pattern followed by this type of schizophrenic during the course of the disorder. During the early stages, process schizophrenics exhibit a slow, insidious loss of interest: general apathy and reduced interest in people and activities. These schizophrenics may appear passive but also nervous, emotional, desperate, and overwhelmed—generally overcome by quiet, tense despair. As the disorder progresses, process schizophrenics begin to undergo personality changes and to act strangely. They also may begin to hear imaginary voices and may seem unusually preoccupied. Inside they feel fear and dread, but on the outside, they show increasingly less initiative and ability to solve their problems.

Schizophrenic symptoms will vary as widely as the personalities of the patients—from quiet to stormy, from very emotional to dull, from outgoing to shy.

Has something changed? What happened to the other kinds of schizophrenia?

You may hear other terms used in the classification of schizophrenia, such as *simple*, *catatonic*, and *hebephrenic*. However, these terms are used much less frequently today because it is difficult to distinguish one type from the others in clinical diagnosis of specific patients. In addition, the symptoms linked with these types of schizophrenia tend to vary widely from patient to patient and within a single patient from time to time. And finally, these descriptive classifications of schizophrenia are not as easy to separate as are the process, acute, and paranoid types.

Simple schizophrenia is a very passive type that seems to deprive the patient of all personality and emotional affect. It is quite rare. A common disorder years ago, catatonic schizophrenia is now also very rare. It is characterized by episodes of rigid posture and immobility called waxy flexibility—with relatively good affect between episodes. Hebephrenic schizophrenics usually exhibit an immature, child-like quality. Characteristically, these patients giggle and act silly, using childish mannerisms in reaction to stress that is disproportionate to the circumstances.

Most patients with these types of disorders are now classified as process schizophrenics because all of them tend to experience a slow onset of the disorder and a gradual loss of emotional affect. They also tend to have common genetic backgrounds.

Another disorder of uncertain cause, now called "borderline syndrome," is no longer classified as one of the schizophrenias by most psychiatrists. It seems to be a distinct disorder and is marked by temporary schizophrenia-like symptoms that show up only when the patient is under stress. Each "borderline" episode promptly disappears when the stress is lifted, seldom lasting more than a few days or weeks. Borderline syndrome is sometimes confused with acute schizophrenia, but it tends to come and go much more frequently than does acute schizophrenia. It also is accompanied by a characteristic black-and-white, angry and depressive type of personality pattern that is usually quite easy to identify. Also separating the two conditions is the fact that an acute schizophrenic episode is always brought on by some enormous stress—from exhaustion, serious family problems, and usually some physical ailments and/or the loss of a loved one—that breaks the patient down. A borderline episode, on the other hand, is always brought on by much milder stress and usually involves a sense of rejection by a loved one in the patient.

What is a nervous breakdown or an emotional illness?

To avoid upsetting the family and patient, many psychiatrists will substitute less stigmatized terms for "schizophrenia" or "mental illness" in describing the patient's illness. Most will say that a patient is emotionally disturbed or that he has a mental condition. They may call the disorder a nervous episode, or say that the patient is emotionally upset. All of these are vague, meaningless terms that could describe *any* important emotional reaction, but which simply do not tell the patient and family what is wrong with the patient. Other psychiatrists may use the popular term *nervous breakdown,* which is not a medical or psychological term at all and can refer to just about any major collapse of nervous, emotional, or mental functions. Still other doctors use the rather general terms *depression* or *emotional depression* to describe a patient's schizophrenia as well as any other mental condition. Unfortunately, the term *depression* can be very misleading because the treatment and typical course of most depressions usually are very different from those of most forms of schizophrenia. As a result, the patient and family who have read about depressions or who know individuals who have been treated for depression through psychiatry or counseling may expect a much more rapid recovery from schizophrenia than usually occurs. Consequently, the patient's family may become unnecessarily discouraged about his or her rate of progress.

Another term, *nerves*, is also used to assuage the fears of patient and family, in this case by differentiating between nervous disorders and the more stigmatized, more serious mental disorders. Patient and family usually show obvious relief when they are told that a condition is "just nerves" and that the patient is not *"crazy."* When the psychiatrist or counselor tries to reassure the patient and family by agreeing that the condition is "just nerves," they are led to think the condition will be cured more easily than is possible—resulting in great disappointment for all. Use of these vague terms often interferes with treatment because the family mistakenly loses faith in the counselor and psychiatrist when the patient fails to recover as rapidly as they expected. To compound the problem, the therapist may be completely perplexed by the situation, because he or she knows the patient's progress is actually fine.

Can you give an example of a typical acute schizophrenic episode?

Joan, age 22, was a pretty, conscientious housewife who was happily married to a letter carrier. She became exhausted during the care of her second baby's colic and came down with one virus after another due to her run-down condition. Frustrated by her condition, her anxious husband became angry with her for not caring for herself better and for always being "too tired" to make love. Finally, still exhausted, Joan began to feel strange electrical sensations run through her body and came to believe that she was being spied on and talked about on the television—that someone was trying to harm her in some vague way that she couldn't understand. She felt keyed up, incapable of sleeping, and finally became totally terrified. Incessantly talkative, crying, and screaming, she was taken to the hospital emergency floor by her alarmed husband. After only two weeks of active treatment and plenty of rest, Joan was back at home feeling fine, caring for her children with help from an aunt who lived next door.

What happens when a typical process schizophrenic becomes ill?

John, age 18, was a recent high school graduate who had been somewhat shy and self-conscious as a boy, but who was also known to be stubborn and even quite temperamental at times. He seemed to lose interest in people and activities around him and became preoccupied with his electronics hobby. He stayed in his room more and more, communicating less and less with his family. He showed reduced interest in finding a job or going to college and never seemed to get around to doing anything for himself. He was irritable when the family mentioned his future.

After months of rapidly increasing isolation and increasing depression, in which he lay in bed awake and daydreaming, he finally started speaking and acting strangely, laughing without mirth or apparent cause. The puzzled family finally had to force him to go to the local mental health clinic, against his will, for diagnosis.

What happens during a typical paranoid schizophrenia breakdown?

Ellen, age 23, was a young, married college student who was extremely bright but who had always tended to be a somewhat self-conscious loner. Her personality was very pleasant, but while at college she became obsessed with her graduate studies to the exclusion of her social life. She also ate poorly, skipped meals, and got little exercise. As the weeks went by she discovered that her power of concentration and her energy were at a low point, and she became more desperate about how slowly her research was proceeding. She was keyed up and tired, and she slept restlessly. She found her interests moving to religion, philosophy, and spiritual matters. Suddenly she was helplessly caught up in the center of a monumental cosmic battle among enormous influences that threatened to destroy the universe. She felt totally inadequate to bear the responsibility of this vague new power, although she enjoyed feeling enormously important and receiving such awesome universal respect. Most of all, she became increasingly terrified of being killed or poisoned by "the other side." Friends began to notice her peculiar delusions, which increased gradually, and after some weeks of worry they finally took her to the emergency floor of the local hospital.

What causes an individual to develop a particular type of schizophrenia?

For years scientists only suspected that schizophrenia runs in families, but studies made recently in Denmark clearly show that both paranoid and process schizophrenia have strong hereditary tendencies. In these studies, adopted children were compared to children raised with their natural parents. The results indicated that the natural children of paranoid and process schizophrenic parents came down with the disorder far more often than did those of normal parents, whether or not these children were raised by natural or foster parents. These results strongly suggest that inheritance was the major cause of these types of schizophrenia. Interestingly, there was no such evidence with respect to the acute type.

Although the connection is not understood, these studies

also revealed that eighty percent of the process schizophrenics who showed no clear pattern of inheritance were born in the winter months!*

Many other studies made throughout the world have also shown that schizophrenia tends to follow genetic lines. For instance, several studies have shown higher rates among affected identical twins than among their nonidentical brothers and sisters and other family members.**

All these study results support the theory that the environment in which schizophrenics are raised, as important as it is, is clearly less important than the inheritance factor or other physical factors in determining the nature and type of schizophrenia.

---

*Recent evidence suggests that there is an association with winter viral diseases and schizophrenia in this group.

***See* "Twin studies" in the Bibliography.

3

Diagnosis and symptoms

How can the family spot schizophrenia?

Diagnosing schizophrenia, as well as naming the specific type, is not an easy task. The disorder takes widely varied forms with different personalities. However, family members may watch for general symptoms and behaviors linked with schizophrenia, so that they may obtain the best available care.

Acute schizophrenia is not as difficult to diagnose as the paranoid and process types. In the period of just a day or two, an apparently normal person explodes into a loud, overactive, literally crazed personality. At this stage of the episode the schizophrenic is a dynamo of overstimulation—prone to wild, strange thoughts and actions, and obviously in need of immediate hospital care. The same symptoms may be caused by a totally different problem, but when these symptoms appear, the family's initial action should be the same—prompt hospitalization and immediate rest for the patient. Sometimes, for instance, those who are allergic to various drugs—alcohol, medications, or hallucinogenic drugs such as LSD—react to them with the signs of an acute schizophrenic episode.

Process and paranoid schizophrenias develop much more slowly and are sometimes more difficult to spot. The first thing the schizophrenic's family might notice is his or her tendency to withdraw from work, school, and family. Second, they will see a definite change in personality, usually toward angry, evasive, suspicious qualities, among other symptoms. Again, it may be difficult for parents of teenagers, in particular, to distinguish signs of schizophrenia from the mental effects of the use of marijuana, "downers," and various other black market drugs. In the case of amphetamines ("speed") use, the symptoms can be indistinguishable at times. Regardless of their cause, these symptoms warrant *immediate professional attention.* Drug abusers usually do not progress to the characteristic, frightening behavior that the schizophrenic develops, which certainly would be noticed by family and doctor in time.

What happens when the schizophrenia progresses past the early stages?

Schoolmates or teachers and coworkers may notice that the schizophrenic's performance is beginning to deteriorate. Family members may watch the person's daily habits changing. For example, schizophrenics often stay awake all night, alone in their rooms, because they cannot sleep. Preferring the quiet nighttime, they effectively turn night into day. Schizophrenics may spend excessive time in bed—not sleeping, but doing very little else. Recovered schizophrenics describe this phase as being in a "pink haze" or a "white cloud," or feeling as if they were passively viewing themselves and the world through some sort of inner television show.

On the other hand, some schizophrenics react to the disorder by becoming uncharacteristically and incessantly active rather than withdrawn. They may become so totally involved in their work and other activities that they are clearly exhausting themselves, yet they still seem constantly keyed up. Occasionally these schizophrenics will show a pressured, frenzied behavior. The particular symptom that makes schizophrenic behavior so strange and frightening to family members is a lack of coherency. The schizophrenic becomes difficult to follow in conversation, acting superior to others, being suddenly and excessively religious, talking about the universe and his or her mission in life—all accompanied by a bizarre, mystical, desperate, vacant, humorless attitude.

Other schizophrenics may gradually sink into the deepest possible depression so that they can hardly move or think. This depression may be very difficult for the family and doctor to distinguish from the severe depression caused by some other disorder.

Schizophrenics may also become irritating and annoying, persistently harassing family members to take one action or another to relieve an impossible situation. They may blame family, employer, or neighbors for whatever they imagine is wrong.

The schizophrenic may exhibit any or all of these symptoms at one point or another in the illness. But whatever the schizophrenic's individual reactions, the hollow, unhappy, out-of-touch, empty tone is always present. Even when he or she appears passive and quiet, the schizophrenic will find it difficult to sleep, to control restlessness, to concentrate, and to function with normal competence—all indicating the disorder to observant family members. Clearly then, any persistent, unexplained change in personality should be investigated by a competent psychiatrist. Even if schizophrenia is not the diagnosis, one of the many other medical conditions that can cause similar behavior may be discovered.

How does the schizophrenic feel?

Schizophrenics usually find it quite difficult to put their inner mental state into words. However, it is clear that every schizophrenic has his or her own special inner world, and it is extremely difficult for others to understand schizophrenics' efforts to talk about how they feel. Schizophrenics sense this bewilderment in others, which only makes them feel more different, alone, apart, and estranged. Not only does the nature of schizophrenia isolate the afflicted person, but it puzzles and frightens those around the schizophrenic, thus further isolating him or her.

In the earliest stage of the illness, the schizophrenic's fear is the predominant feeling. Schizophrenics who are beginning to break down always feel overwhelmed with anxiety and overwhelmed by their lives. They feel they cannot cope. Fear of losing touch with familiar things, with familiar security, bothers them. They always feel that they are in a fearful dream world, in a separate existence. Schizophrenia is a very unpleasant disorder.

Schizophrenics often feel mildly physically ill as well, but their main concern is dealing with the bizarre unreality of their lives. The disorder feels more like a dream than a physical sickness to the schizophrenic. When nonschizophrenics dream, they cannot tell they are dreaming; they believe in the dream while it is occurring and realize it wasn't real only when they wake up. Schizophrenics feel a similar effect, except they are dreaming while awake. They are aware of and capable of remembering what is really going on, but whatever they see, feel, and think is a different reality from which they cannot awaken. In many cases, schizophrenics may not even know that they have been captured by this dream world. However, by the time they are first seen by a professional, the vast majority of schizophrenics know they have a mental illness.

There are several books, including the popular *I Never Promised You a Rose Garden*, in which schizophrenics have written about themselves during their illnesses and recoveries.

What is this schizophrenic dream world like?

One schizophrenic said that as he became ill his room gradually became the bedroom of a simple, humble king, glowing with an unusually bright and dazzling light. Although she hadn't really changed, his wife mysteriously became a queen. At the same time, this man felt an underlying fear of potential danger constantly lurking around him, which he did not understand. Everything was the same, yet different—exciting, frightening, strange and real, but not as it was before. The man himself changed, too, into a new, more important person. Realizing many more abilities and powers than he had known before, but being important, he was more vulnerable to his enemies, who might try to hurt him.

Unlike the exciting drama that the schizophrenic writers describe in their books, most schizophrenics don't really have a great deal to report about their illness. Their new lives are dull, frightening, threatening, and strange. The dream—really a nightmare—is boring and routine with few interesting details, like most of their real, unhappy, boring lives. These hallucinations are just part of the dream and can be compared to the hallucinations that naturally accompany normal people's dreams. Schizophrenics may hear voices commanding them to do this or that, or voices or other sounds calling their names, or vague or threatening references to themselves over the radio or television—all parts of their daily true-to-life dream.

Although they often hear voices, schizophrenics seldom have visual hallucinations, which commonly suggest a drug reaction rather than schizophrenia. When the schizophrenic disorder is active, schizophrenics tend, rather, to mistake what they see. If they are driving, for instance, the road and trees may look as if they were closing in on them. Bushes or sky may seem to be moving or beckoning to them. The line in the middle of the road may appear to waver and lead them to eternity. When they look at their reflection in a mirror, they often see a face that seems older, younger, thinner, or like a witch or other personality. Objects may appear unnaturally narrow or wide, huge or tiny. Time may seem to speed up or slow down. Coordination of hands or legs may seem to deteriorate. Schizophrenics feel unable to think, concentrate, or remember as well as they did in the past.

Schizophrenia affects all portions of the brain; it upsets all thinking, feeling, and functioning of the schizophrenic during the actively sick period.

What can family members do when they think someone has schizophrenia?

Obviously, it is not easy to deal with people who are living in a nightmarish dream world and whose judgment, logic, and performance have deteriorated. Family efforts to try to talk to them and reassure them are usually unsuccessful, because schizophrenics misinterpret the meaning of what is being said. How can one reason with someone who is dreaming? To make communication even more difficult, schizophrenics may not appear to want help, because in their dream the world is crazy, not they. But they are almost always grateful when treatment brings them back to reality—depending on the reality they come back to.

The first step the family should take is to get the person to a good psychiatrist as soon as possible. Although schizophrenia usually is not an emergency, it could be. If the inner dream is a spy story in which the hero is supposed to take poison to prevent the bad guys from getting vital information from him, the schizophrenic may end up trying to harm himself. And he could succeed while the family is deciding whether or not to consult a psychiatrist. So it usually pays to act promptly. Generally, schizophrenia does not tend to improve without treatment.

How does the family find a psychiatrist?

Don't waste time calling a psychiatrist if the schizophrenic seems to be in trouble. Immediately take the person to the emergency floor of the local hospital, where he or she will be given first aid and made comfortable. If the patient does not agree to go to the hospital, call your family doctor, the local mental health center, the police, or a social worker for help.

The first job is to protect the life of the patient, not to worry about stigma, false loyalty, or retaliation on the part of anyone involved. After the patient has been given medication to calm him or her down, and/or is hospitalized, the family and patient can take the time to find the best psychiatrist in the area for a complete diagnosis and treatment plan.

What do you do when there is no emergency but the patient refuses to seek a professional diagnosis?

This is a common situation that calls for holding strategy sessions with someone in your area who knows something about mental illnesses. Consult your family doctor, mental health clinic, a good psychiatrist, or a social worker who is knowledgeable in the field. It is a good idea to gather all the adults in the family for a discussion or two on getting the patient the diagnostic workup that he or she needs. Each situation—each area, each patient, each family—is unique and must be handled locally and individually. The family should persist in its efforts to get the patient a diagnostic workup. This may prove to be extremely frustrating because it often means dealing not only with a difficult patient and many family problems but also with a bureaucracy of various community agencies and the medical "establishment," sometimes without finding anyone who seems to understand the problem.

Where are schizophrenic evaluations made?

These days, schizophrenics may not have to go to a mental

hospital for diagnosis. Many general hospitals will take a patient for evaluation, because the patient can usually be calmed down within an hour or two through injections of an antischizophrenic medication in a private office or on the emergency floor. Often, the patient can simply go to the hospital for outpatient tests.

It may be advisable to admit some patients to a regular hospital bed or a general hospital psychiatric unit. More community mental health centers are now sprouting up throughout the country in place of the old state mental hospitals. These new mental health centers are usually much smaller and more efficiently operated than state hospitals, but they often lack the essential diagnostic laboratory and X ray facilities, and they are often short on psychiatrists.

Sometimes the best spot for evaluation is where the best psychiatrist is, regardless of the facility. Even when a clinic bears a famous name, there is no guarantee that it will offer excellent diagnoses in mental illness. A psychiatrist's community reputation for the treatment of schizophrenia, *among families of schizophrenics in the community*, is often a more reliable indicator of competence than a worldwide reputation. In addition, a psychiatrist who is reputable and competent in one field, such as psychotherapy, may not do well at all in the diagnosis and treatment of mental illnesses.

Is putting the schizophrenic in a hospital a "commitment"?

Patients are committed only when they enter a private hospital, community mental health center, or state mental hospital against their will. The vast majority of patients sign themselves into these facilities on their own, thus avoiding an involuntary commitment. Entering voluntarily is better for everybody. Patients thus protect themselves against any subsequent legal problems, besides leaving better feelings within the family and among the family, the doctor, and the treatment staff afterward. In general hospitals, of course, the patient is nearly always admitted like any other patient—with no strings attached.

How do we know that the patient is getting good care?

This is an important problem. Just as the family that is new to schizophrenia knows little about its diagnosis and treatment, many other people know little about the disorder, including, unhappily, many physicians, nurses, psychiatrists, social workers, and psychologists. The diagnosis and treatment of schizophrenia is just emerging from the "Dark Ages." There are relatively few—perhaps a thousand or so—private specialists in mental illness in the United States and Canada. The quality of diagnosis in various general hospitals, mental health centers, and other institutions varies enormously, from superb to very poor. In most cases, the family that is new to the problems of diagnosis and treatment soon encounters this unfortunate ignorance.

How do we find the best psychiatrist?

The best source is the telephone. You can call your local schizophrenia or mental health association, or, better yet, call the local Alliance for the Mentally Ill in your area because this group usually already knows who the best local doctors and counselors are. Ask the family doctor or the hospital chief of staff to recommend a good psychiatrist. Call a social worker and, if you can, get in touch with other families of schizophrenic patients and ask them which psychiatrist they found best in the community. These families often have been through the whole trial-and-error process and may save the schizophrenic and family an enormous amount of time and money by pointing to the best schizophrenia psychiatrist in the community. Many cities have day-care centers for the mentally ill, where you might find families who are familiar with the best psychiatrists and facilities for treatment.

In the search, the family should always ask specifically for a schizophrenia or mental illness specialist. When you find a psychiatrist, do not be shy about asking right away whether he or she is a specialist in this area. Today, psychiatry is still roughly split into the psychotherapists, or "talking" psychiatrists, and the medical types who tend to talk less and treat patients more medically. At first, the family needs the second type, the medical specialist, so that the diagnosis and treatment plan will be done properly the first time. Later, it may be important for the family and patient to consult the talking type of psychiatrist, but only after the schizophrenia itself is under control and the schizophrenic has returned to reality. Talking therapies generally work poorly when the schizophrenia is active. (*See* Dr. Manshreck's article in the Bibliography.)

What happens if the patient ends up in the hospital or with a doctor in whom the family does not have confidence?

As soon as the patient is under a reasonable amount of control, the patient or family should get a second opinion from the schizophrenia specialist they found through all their telephone calls. *It is totally, absolutely, and completely vital to be sure of the diagnosis when the patient first breaks down.* Many families have experienced the trauma of running from place to place without knowing what they are doing, watching the schizophrenic's condition get rapidly poorer through incorrect treatment, and still not realizing what the best treatment is. Then when they do find the best treatment, they can no longer afford it. Patients and families *will* find what they need in a competent schizophrenia specialist's office. Unfortunately, there is no national listing of schizophrenia specialists in the United States at this time.

Never be afraid to seek a second opinion. If your doing so hurts the feelings of the first psychiatrist, you probably need a new doctor anyway. All doctors are trained to use consultations. They are public servants, and the *patient* should always be their first concern. (For information on handling doctors, see Chapter 12.) The family should get a second opinion if anyone has any doubts.

How does one determine whether the patient has had a complete workup?

Ask yourself the following questions. Did the doctor or staff take a complete history on the patient and family, including mental, physical, and family disorders and alcoholism? Did the doctor really get to know the patient and spend time with him or her? Was a complete blood and urine examination done? Did the patient go through a blood profile, a thyroid test, and a complete physical and neurological exam? Did the doctor take the appropriate X rays and do a brain wave test?

Today, the CT scan ("CAT Scan"), an incredibly wonderful instrument, is painless and accurate in providing an excellent electronic picture of the brain. It is now becoming almost a necessary part of the routine for patients with mental illness when there is any diagnostic problem.

The one big problem in the diagnosis of schizophrenia is that no definitive blood test or any *certain* laboratory test proves that one variety or another of the schizophrenias is present. A number of objective laboratory tests are available, but they are still in the research stage and are not really useful in clinical practice. It should not be long, however, before accurate laboratory tests are available. Until then, reasonable certainty of the diagnosis is established by the use of a combination of basic medical and psychiatric symptoms, psychological tests, and laboratory tests.

Why is it so important to get the correct diagnosis at first?

Not only is it expensive and time-consuming for the patient and family to get the wrong treatment for a misdiagnosed disorder, but there are just so many mental disorders that can *appear* to be schizophrenia. Brain tumor, drug reactions, endocrine gland problems (thyroid, pituitary, pancreas, adrenal, and others), head injury, meningitis, encephalitis, birth problems, and numerous nutritional disorders are just a few of the possibilities.

A good diagnosis also involves identifying specific problems—physical, marital, work-related, social, economic—that the individual patient and family may have. It is a totally different treatment problem, for instance, if the schizophrenic is a wife with two children than if her working husband has the schizophrenia. It is different for an orphaned sixteen-year-old student than for an alcoholic parent in a single-parent family. And it is different for a paraplegic living in a remote farm area than for an inner-city member of a minority group. It even makes a great big deal of difference whether the patient and family are rich or poor! Thus, tailoring treatment to fit in with highly individualized circumstances is a true test of a good evaluation and treatment plan.

4

Treatment

What type of general treatment is appropriate for schizophrenia?

Like diabetes, schizophrenia requires several basic types of treatment, and for the best results they all must be used simultaneously. First of all, the schizophrenic and family need to learn the vital dos and don'ts of a healthy lifestyle, which are detailed in Chapter 5. Second, someone needs to counsel the schizophrenic, to talk to the person and find out who he or she is, what he or she is like, what problems the person has, what he or she wants out of life, and so on. Someone also needs to talk to the family, who, for the purposes of this book, will be those the patient lives with. The counselor must find out about their problems and what they want out of life as well. The family and patient should almost always have the same counselor, to avoid misunderstandings stemming from one-sided points of view. It takes working together, under one counselor who won't take sides, to carry out the treatment. Finally, most schizophrenics feel better, sharper, more alert, and closer to reality when taking some form of medication.

What other treatments may be necessary?

The majority of all schizophrenics break down during their late teens and early twenties, before they have learned working skills, so they probably will need vocational training. Also, schizophrenics who have regressed must become socially active again. They need to have fun and excitement, to learn to live normally.

Some schizophrenics also have special problems—physical disorders such as blood sugar or allergy problems, physical handicaps and other disorders that complicate the treatment of schizophrenia. No doubt, the worst of these problems is abuse of such drugs as alcohol, caffeine, and marijuana. Schizophrenics must stop taking all nonprescription drugs, because they increase the adverse effects of the illness.

In a way, the main treatment actually consists of helping the schizophrenic return to a normal, healthy life. He or she must recover good health before resuming the maturing process. All physical and mental handicaps slow down or stop normal maturing. When an individual fails to mature, mental stagnation sets in.

Which is the most important type of treatment?

No single treatment is more important than the others. Like links in a chain, all the treatments are essential; when a single link is missing, the chain is broken and ineffective. For some schizophrenics, the key to recovery may lie in correcting a food allergy such as a wheat or milk allergy or an environmental allergy such as the gas furnace in the home. For other schizophrenics, that key might lie in a family member's giving up drinking. The point is that the patient and family must amass a thorough knowledge of the major problems that may be encountered, and then they must correct every one of them. With a little experience, this can be easier than it may seem at first.

Why are medications used in the treatment of schizophrenia?

Schizophrenia medications calm down the overactive brain cells of the schizophrenic. This brings the whole brain back to more normal functioning—the person feels more relaxed, less afraid, more confident, and more capable of concentrating. The use of schizophrenic medications has revolutionized the treatment of schizophrenia. Very few schizophrenics stay in hospitals or institutions for long periods anymore. Like the TB hospitals of years ago, mental hospitals are rapidly emptying, and many have closed—mainly due to these effective new medications.

Which kind of medication should be used for each type of schizophrenia?

There is still no reliable method for determining which medication will be the best one for a particular schizophrenic. Coming up with the proper medications in the correct dosage for a particular person is still a matter of trial and error. The patient and family will often need to be patient while the doctor tries various combinations of medication and dosage. The correct dosage is one that brings the person back to *normal* thinking, mood, and sleep patterns, yet does not "drug" or "zombie" him through excess. Antipsychotic drugs do not automatically sedate schizophrenics. With the right dosage, they are more alert, can concentrate better, and do everything better. Complaints about these medications are common, but only because the schizophrenic is overmedicated, a problem that can be solved easily.

Those interested in the names, actions, and side effects of these medications can obtain them from a psychiatrist or pharmacist. A medication can have all sorts of effects on various people, so side effects should be discussed with the psychiatrist to assure that the correct medication and dosage are found as quickly as possible.

Modern medications are very strong and have a number of side effects. For instance, aspirin has at least four different effects: It reduces pain, but also reduces inflammation and fever and "thins" the blood. Like aspirin, the antipsychotics also have several actions. Fortunately, all antischizophrenic medications produce roughly the same major side effects. It is very important for the patient and family to recognize this, because the schizophrenic will almost always feel these side effects to some degree.

What are these side effects?

The most common side effect is a harmless physical restlessness, an inner nervous anxiety or tension that is relieved by moving around, especially by walking or riding in a car. It is called akathesia and is easily relieved by an antidote, a so-called anti-Parkinson medication. The problem with this side effect is that it feels somewhat like the anxiety, fear, and tension of schizophrenia. If a mistake is made by the patient, family, or doctor in spotting reactions to medications, the doctor probably will increase the medication, which only increases the restlessness. If the schizophrenic just can't sit still or is always jiggling the legs like a teenager, then he or she may have akathesia, which should be relieved promptly.

A second side effect is a rigid muscle problem called dystonia. The back of the patient's legs—and, later, the arms, back, and neck—may feel and appear tight. The patient walks around as if the neck were stiff and may even drool a little. Relaxed expressions never appear on the schizophrenic's face. The schizophrenic feels stiff all over.

Sometimes the head is tilted to one side (torticollis), the jaws are stiff, or the eyes roll upward (oculogyric crises). These symptoms too, are relieved by the anti-Parkinson medication.

What about the "zombie" effect that everybody talks about?

A third side effect is the well-known "zombie" effect called akinesia. The schizophrenic becomes much quieter, less active, and less interested in things and shows fewer normal emotions than before the medication was used. Internally, the patient does not feel physically uncomfortable, as with akathesia or dystonia. This "zombie" akinesia is a sneaky, gradual side effect, and the lack of energy and initiative is often difficult to distinguish from the depression that often accompanies schizophrenia. However, when the schizophrenic is depressed, he or she usually feels worse in the morning and feels better as the day goes on. Further, the patient actually suffers from these hopeless depressed feelings. However, with akinesia, the schizophrenic feels reasonably well and is not subject to mood changes during the day. Mild cases of akinesia are also relieved by anti-Parkinson antidotes, and more severe cases are relieved by lowering or discontinuing the dosage of the medication itself.

Unfortunately, many doctors—even psychiatrists—may not notice or may misinterpret these side effects. The patient and family may need to be firm in telling the doctor or counselor if one of these effects is noted. It might help if you can use the technical terms for them!

What minor side effects should the schizophrenic expect?

When first taking medications, all schizophrenics notice some drowsiness, distraction, and an increased tendency to sleep. Occasionally they will feel some dryness of the mouth, slight constipation, a stuffy nose or a mild headache in the morning. These side effects should all disappear within a few days; if they do not, it usually means the schizophrenic is taking more medication than he or she needs.

What about the uncommon side effects?

Occasionally a patient will become supersensitive to sun. The face, hands, and other areas where the skin is exposed will get sore and swollen after only a short period in the sun. Usually, a switch in medication is all that is needed.

A second serious but relatively uncommon complication can result from extended use of these medications and is called tardive dyskinesia. It is a peculiar, embarrassing disorder in which involuntary movements of the mouth, lips, tongue, arms, and hips plague the schizophrenic. *Patient and family should be thoroughly familiar with this important disorder from discussions with their doctor because it is easily managed in the early stage but hard to treat later on.* In my practice, I have never had a patient who was taking the multi-vitamin "horse pills" that I prescribe—one or two a day—come down with T.D.*

What else should the patient and family know about medications?

One important discovery in schizophrenic treatment is long-acting medications for patients who have problems with taking medications regularly. In pill or injection form, a single dose may last from seven to twenty-one days, so the patient can make fewer trips to the office and need not remember to take the medication every day. Also, for some reason, many patients prefer taking injections to having to remember to take pills at home.

It is also important for the family to realize that as the schizophrenia improves, more side effects may appear, especially a drowsy, drugged effect with an I-can't-wait-to-get-to-bed-at-night feeling. This is actually a good sign, because it

---

**See* Chapter 6 on nutrition.

is caused by an improvement in the schizophrenia, which lowers the schizophrenic's medication requirement. Patient and family should be sure the doctor reduces the dosage when this happens.

Will the schizophrenic ever be able to stop taking medications altogether?

Like a diabetic being treated with insulin, the schizophrenic may or may not be able to abstain totally from medications. Much depends on how carefully the patient follows the dos and don'ts discussed in the next chapter—plus just plain luck! If the patient is lucky, he or she will have a mild case of schizophrenia combined with a pleasant lifestyle and may be able to discontinue the medications for long periods of time. Regardless, as the schizophrenia improves, these doses of medication are gradually lowered, which means fewer pills and fewer side effects.

Usually, one of two reasons causes the schizophrenic to push seriously to get off the medications. The first is that he is feeling unpleasant side effects from the medications, a problem that should be solved promptly; the other is an intense desire to feel cured of the disorder. The second reason is a normal, healthy reaction to any illness. However, the most effective reaction for both the patient and the family is to help the patient learn to accept schizophrenia as a long-term disorder that cannot be cured but, rather, managed. If the schizophrenic does not accept this fact, the schizophrenic, the family, and the doctor are likely to get involved in an unhappy tussle over the medication.

Are schizophrenia medications habit-forming or addictive? Do medications stop working after a while?

No. None of the schizophrenia medications is addictive. And once the medications work, they continue to work. If a relapse occurs while the patient is on medication, it is caused by something else, most often by a failure to follow the dos and don'ts, by a medication side effect, or by increased stress on the patient which calls for at least a temporary increase in medication.

5

Dos and don'ts of daily living

What is the most important part of the schizophrenic's daily routine?

As discussed in Chapter 4, all parts of the schizophrenic's treatment are equally important in producing the desired result. The same is true of the schizophrenic's daily routine; all of its parts must be adhered to in order to keep the patient well. However, if there is any single daily habit that is more important than the others, it is sleep. For some reason, schizophrenics require more sleep than nonschizophrenics. Schizophrenics simply do not feel right unless they get the sleep they need. It is easy to determine how much sleep a schizophrenic requires by averaging the amount of time spent sleeping over two or three nights, letting the patient awaken spontaneously each morning. Some schizophrenics seem to need as much as eleven hours of sleep a night, which can be quite a problem if they are married, if they pursue late-night activities, or if they are particularly busy otherwise. Excessive sleep also can mean that the medication dosage is too high, so be sure to report this problem to the physician. Whatever the individual need, *every schizophrenic should get at least eight hours of sleep every night.*

What does it mean when the schizophrenic finds it difficult to fall asleep?

Difficulty in falling asleep is the most reliable early sign of schizophrenic relapse. It typically strikes when the schizophrenic gets too keyed up during the day, and even when he or she sleeps fitfully and then dozes late the next morning, the patient never really sleeps deeply. The keyed-up condition usually persists through the night and into the next day.

What should the schizophrenic do to counteract this problem?

When the schizophrenic sleeps poorly one night he or she should slow the pace during the day in order to be relaxed by bedtime. When slowing down doesn't work—and for patients in very upset, keyed-up states—the patient should arrange with the doctor for extra medications to take that night to be sure to resume regular sleep habits. Careful monitoring of sleep is especially important because schizophrenics tend to become exhausted or keyed up quite easily—a sure sign of trouble ahead if not corrected.

What types of things can overstimulate the schizophrenic?

One of the most common causes of overstimulation is ingestion of caffeine.* Caffeine is probably the least known

---

**See* Caffeine section in the Bibliography.

but most vital taboo in the treatment of schizophrenia. During the rehabilitation period, most schizophrenics cannot even drink one cup of coffee without feeling a noticeable disorganizing effect on their thinking, in addition to overstimulation. Caffeine also directly disturbs sleep in schizophrenics by stimulating the sleep centers in the brain. Schizophrenics' oversensitivity to stimulants is apparently due to the oversensitivity of their brain cells. Schizophrenics who insist on drinking coffee and other caffeine-containing beverages and medications require much more medication to balance their moods. Unfortunately, extra medications often increase side effects enough to "zombie" the patient noticeably. Every stimulant worsens schizophrenic symptoms. *Schizophrenics should not use stimulants of any kind.*

Besides coffee, what foods or beverages contain caffeine or other stimulants?

There is caffeine in cocoa, hot chocolate, tea, and soft drinks such as cola beverages (regular and sugar-free), Dr. Pepper, and Moxie. Cocoa, hot chocolate, and tea also contain other stimulants besides caffeine. Freshly brewed coffee has the greatest stimulant effect—about twice as much as a cup of tea—and hot cocoa, chocolate, and the colas have smaller but nonetheless important amounts. Medications such as Anacin, Empirin, APC, and many asthma and cold preparations also contain caffeine and other stimulants. Some of the most potent stimulants are those in diet drugs. No schizophrenic should take any over-the-counter or prescription medication without carefully reading the labels or asking the doctor or pharmacist whether stimulants are present.

What beverages can the schizophrenic drink safely?

Decaffeinated coffee, very weak tea, many diet drinks, and fruit juices are usually safe. Cold spring water is the most neglected and best drink available for schizophrenics.

What other influences overstimulate the schizophrenic?

One stimulant activity is a fast pace of living. Schizophrenics sometimes rush around too much trying to get too much done too quickly, getting involved in the "rat race." Many schizophrenics who have been sick for a while and then have improved try to make up for lost time. They get so involved in working long hours that they get exhausted and keyed up. Schizophrenics need to practice a comfortable, easygoing lifestyle that they can sustain over their lifetime.

Another activity that can overstimulate schizophrenics is very heavy exercise just before bedtime. Apparently this doesn't allow the schizophrenic to calm down before trying to go to sleep. While the same problem does touch non-schizophrenics, the schizophrenic's metabolism often takes longer to slow down, so that this is a fairly common and difficult problem. For schizophrenics, exercise is best taken in the morning or afternoon.

How do alcoholic beverages affect schizophrenics?

Unlike stimulants, alcoholic beverages temporarily make the schizophrenic feel relaxed and confident. In addition, moderate amounts of alcohol usually provoke few hangover-type aftereffects. So the schizophrenic naturally believes that alcoholic beverages are reasonably safe to drink. However, it is interesting that the schizophrenic suffers the unfortunate effects one or two days later, long after anyone might expect a hangover. After this delay, the most significant effects are the mildly depressed, logy, anxious, tense, irritable moods, which, in turn, are almost always followed by the overstimulated, nervous state. This, of course, is followed by sleep problems.

After ingesting a *substantial* amount of beer, wine, or liquor, the schizophrenic may react so severely that the milder hangover effects are accompanied by hallucinations and delusions. Most schizophrenics do not realize that these delayed effects are caused by alcohol because the symptoms appear so late. Thus the schizophrenic is likely to connect the effect with a more recent cause. Schizophrenics who drink daily invariably have much worse symptoms than they would without drinking. Of course, these people may not be aware of the worsening effect because they don't remain sober for the full five or six days required to get over the alcohol effects. So, another don't is, *Schizophrenics should not drink alcoholic beverages.*

What are the effects of marijuana?

Marijuana makes almost all schizophrenics anxious, restless, and paranoid. A similar drug, hashish ("hash"), is like concentrated marijuana; it has similar effects but is stronger. Unlike alcohol, marijuana's effects occur within a few hours of smoking, so most schizophrenics quickly decide they don't want to smoke it again. Some schizophrenics feel none of the typical side effects of marijuana, even when they smoke a lot. They do, however, always become seriously "do-nothing"—passive, irritable, and tending to blame others for their inactivity. Usually, these schizophrenics will see nothing wrong in their inactivity, anyway. These schizophrenics are also difficult to treat because they must stop smoking marijuana entirely, which usually is the last thing they want to do. It's really difficult to convince schizophrenics who really enjoy marijuana and suffer no bad side effects from it—therefore feeling no pain or discomfort—that they must stop using it. But every effort should be made to stop the schizophrenic's use of marijuana.

Cigarettes contain nicotine. Is nicotine a problem?

In most cases the mild stimulant effects from the nicotine in cigarettes seems to have no specific or serious effects on schizophrenics. Some schizophrenics are allergic to cigarette smoke, which will provoke the same type of reaction as do other food and pollen allergens. No matter how difficult it is, schizophrenics who are not completely recovering should stop smoking for at least two months because smoking can be a problem in some cases. On the other hand, it is now clear that cigarette smoking causes many physical disorders—heart attacks, cancer, emphysema—and is generally detrimental to one's health. Hopefully, even if just for good general health, schizophrenics and family members will all stop smoking eventually.

What can be done for the schizophrenic who cannot, or will not, stop smoking?

Not everyone can give up everything all at once. One of the best compromises for schizophrenics who are putting their energies into practicing the dos and don'ts of good health is to switch from higher tar-and-nicotine cigarettes to the lowest tar-and-nicotine cigarette, "Box" Carleton. Switching to very low tar-and-nicotine cigarettes clearly and promptly improves the health of heavy cigarette smokers. They cough and wheeze less and have fewer stains on their fingers. An encouraging note: As difficult as it may be to make the switch at first, many of those changing to the low tar-and-nicotine cigarettes say it usually takes no more than a week to ten days to come to *prefer* these cigarettes, because they feel so much better. Of course, it's a shame for the schizophrenic and family to spend so much energy and time helping a patient recover from schizophrenia only to become physically ill from cigarettes!

6

Dos and don'ts of nutrition

Is there anything special schizophrenics should know about diet?

Yes. Much exciting new research has shown that there can be a wide variety of nutritional hazards for schizophrenics, and there are some important guidelines for optimum diet. Before being concerned with these special features, however, it is only common sense that schizophrenics start by following a simple, healthy diet consisting of a reasonable balance of carbohydrates, proteins, fats, fiber, vitamins, and minerals. Plenty of fruits, salads, and unprocessed natural foods are clearly important. Generally, schizophrenics seem to fare better with a reasonably low carbohydrate diet, which is doubly difficult because today's diet tends to be too high in carbohydrates such as sugars and starches—sweets, bakery goods, and junk foods. Schizophrenics should eat three to four meals of approximately the same size at the same time every day (breakfast is the most important meal of the day and it is often ignored). Fad diets or intensive reducing diets are nutritionally unsound because they put intense stimulating stress on the schizophrenic. Actually these should be avoided by anyone who suffers from *any* long term physical disorder.

Why do you say schizophrenics should eat unprocessed foods?

Because unprocessed foods do not contain the countless additives—food colors, preservatives, hormones, chemicals—which can be toxic to anyone, but are believed to be especially toxic to nutritionally vulnerable schizophrenics. Unprocessed foods also contain "micro-nutrients," many of which are necessary to good nutrition and are often removed in food processing.

What do you mean by "micro-nutrients"?

Biochemists have pointed out that tomatoes have about 25,000 different chemicals in them, humans about 100,000. Among these naturally occurring compounds it is probable that there are many as yet undiscovered important nutrients called "micro-nutrients" that the human body actually requires. The heating, macerating, and pulverizing of food and the chemical alterations of its nutritional value by additives, preservatives, colorings, texturizers, hormones, and fillers are believed by some to be destroying essential nutrients. Also, there is now massive evidence that some of these chemicals harm the body through their cancer-causing, toxic, and allergic effects. In addition, when these chemicals are added to natural food substances, new compounds formed by the chemical interactions may also have harmful effects.

But aren't there naturally occurring toxic chemicals?

Yes. Green apples, toxic mushrooms, and poison ivy are good examples of naturally occurring toxic substances which we all have to avoid. It must be remembered that each human has a highly individualized chemistry. For instance, while most individuals can eat tomatoes in any amount, some people react to them as if they were eating a toxic substance, encountering such symptoms as nausea, headache, arthritic symptoms, and cold sores. Some people get hayfever from pollens and house dust while others don't. Others are allergic to feathers. There are even at least two reports of women who are allergic to their husbands! So each individual has to learn what he can eat and breathe and what he must avoid. Another important point is that over the millions of years of the evolving of nature, the human body has learned to manage—to naturally detoxify—naturally occurring substances. But it has not yet learned how to handle some of the thousands of new artificial chemicals being spewed into the air, soil, and water, as well as those being put directly into foods. Some people cannot stand tobacco smoke, some get headaches from paint fumes, and some choke from hairsprays. Many get foggy, confused, and even hallucinate from certain of these substances. As a result, the body reacts to these new substances by mild or severe symptoms of poisoning. Of course, any of these reactions can worsen schizophrenia, because most of them, in one degree or another, affect the brain.

Do vitamins affect these toxic reactions?

Probably. There is good evidence that when larger-than-usual doses of some vitamins are added to the diet, the body can "detoxify" the natural or artificial toxic substances much more easily—the detoxifying process itself using up the vitamins in the body. For instance, when a certain TB drug is given, it has been found that it is necessary to add vitamin B_6, which not only detoxifies this medicine but also prevents depletion of B_6 in the body due to the medicine.

Why should schizophrenics eat a low carbohydrate diet?

Many schizophrenics seem to have an unstable blood sugar metabolism, which can result in such symptoms as mood change, irritability, and poor concentration. Thus, a large intake of carbohydrates only adds to the schizophrenic's thinking disorder. A high carbohydrate diet also tends to cause overweight, which is just as depressing to a self-conscious schizophrenic as it is to anyone else!

What other dietary pitfalls should schizophrenics be aware of?

One of them is copper. High copper levels have been shown to be associated with nervous and mental disorders. Today's plumbing is primarily copper, which dissolves in very small amounts in tap water. (Copper produces that blue-green stain under a dripping faucet.) High copper levels have been produced by estrogen in women who take birth control pills and have been associated with vitamin preparations with substantial amounts of copper in them. Drinking water should come only from the cold water faucet and only after it has been run for a while to clean out stagnant water. (Hot water dissolves a little more copper than cold.) Although copper is an important essential mineral in body functioning, copper depletion is extremely rare. Zinc supplements are believed by a few to help control blood copper levels when they are unavoidably high.

A second pitfall to be aware of is lead. Lead comes from automobile exhausts, lead paint, storage batteries, and from various manufacturing processes which contaminate the air and drinking water. Precautionary blood or hair lead levels should be taken in people who live in the city, near busy highways or dumps, or close to certain manufacturing areas.

I've read so much about megavitamins; what are the facts about vitamins for schizophrenics?

Many schizophrenics clearly have unusual and vulnerable

metabolisms. Higher than usual doses of some vitamins are believed to help stabilize metabolic processes by normalizing a variety of defective enzyme reactions that schizophrenics seem to have. Moderate doses of some vitamins might be effective in this way, because they comprise the basic molecular building blocks for many enzyme molecules. While much research remains to be done in this field, it is clear, especially in the early years of the schizophrenic illness, vitamin and mineral supplements can be beneficial in the treatment of the basic chemical defects in schizophrenia. Some vitamins and minerals apparently help prevent reactions from environmental toxins mentioned previously through support of the body's natural detoxifying system. They also help with disorders of vitamin utilization, such as poor absorption in the intestines, or in metabolic or dietary deficiency states. At the very least, every schizophrenic who does not get entirely better should consult a skilled nutritionist. For those who aren't able to get a nutritionist in the immediate future two good wide spectrum vitamin supplements are VM 75 (Solgar, available at many health food stores) and Ultramega (GNC stores) at a dose of one or two capsules a day.

What is orthomolecular psychiatry?

Orthomolecular psychiatry is a branch of medicine designed to treat mental disorders by two basic processes. First, it attempts to remove toxic influences from the body and brain, and, second, it attempts to add appropriate corrective nutrient molecules in optimum concentrations to provide the best biochemical balances for good metabolic functioning of the body and brain. It is a legitimate pioneering medical movement with many theories about the use of vitamins, minerals, lecithin, choline, lithium, nutritional disease prevention, and environmental and ecological treatments. Because its whole concept is different in some ways from traditional medical styles, it is still controversial. Unfortunately, few physicians have seen the amazing effects of a good clinical ecologist's treatment (they treat allergies, sensitivities, and food addictions) or the bouncy vitality of a recovered schizophrenic through orthomolecular techniques. Further research and increasing contact with local physicians may combine to produce full acceptance of this branch of medicine. A majority of schizophrenia specialists are not orthomolecular psychiatrists, and there is no reason their treatment cannot be supplemented by nutritionists, clinical ecologists, and the guidelines in this book.

Do large doses of vitamins cause any side effects?

They can happen. Vitamin D in excessive doses causes kidney stones and hardening of the arteries in some cases. Vitamin A can cause skin problems, congenital malformations, and blood and liver abnormalities. Without supervision by a competent nutritionally trained professional, the dose of Vitamin A should not exceed 25,000 units a day, or vitamin D 800–1,000 international units a day. Vitamin B_3 (niacin), especially when taken on an empty stomach, can cause flushing, sweating, and fast heartbeat, but these effects are harmless. Excessive calcium supplements, especially when combined with vitamin D, can be hazardous. Otherwise, the usual vitamin and mineral supplements can be taken in reasonable quantities without risk. Trace minerals when taken in excess can be poisonous.

If the basic orthomolecular nutritional approach works so well, why haven't I heard more about it?

Relative to other forms of schizophrenia treatment, the nutritional approach (carefully omitting toxic foods, beverages, tobacco, and environmental allergens, and adding nutrients like vitamins and minerals in larger than average doses) is "new". The way people are raised today on television commercials of sugar-coated breakfast cereals, nutritional treatment of disease is often simply hard to believe! It is difficult for new approaches that go against the grain of our basic ideas to gain public acceptance (for instance, that good nutrition is vital in the treatment of schizophrenia).

Why don't some doctors "believe" in the new approach?

The only possible answer to this is that either they haven't tried it or they have been so blinded by their medical training that they cannot believe what they are seeing if they *do* try it! When properly done, results are so prompt and dramatic that no competent observer could possibly miss the effects. The sensible nutritional approach of leaving out alcohol, coffee, marijuana, tobacco, and wheat-corn-milk products and taking moderate doses of water soluble vitamins is absolutely harmless and can hardly be considered hazardous to the health by any physician regardless of his background. The question often asked in orthomolecular circles is: "If it is harmless, and previous treatments of other types have not worked or have been only mildly effective, why not give the nutritional approach a try?" Of course, the point is that this approach, as a part of the total schizophrenia treatment, will help a lot at the least, and it may actually save someone's life.

Does the nutritional approach always work?

Nothing *always* works. But it is hard to believe any person's health couldn't be improved by leaving out alcohol, coffee, tobacco, and junk foods and by adding judicious amounts of vitamins and minerals. Not all schizophrenics do have allergies (see Chapter VII) or major nutritional deficiencies, so that the common, dramatic results of nutritional treatment do not occur in everyone. However, the *usual* reasons for lack of substantial improvement through nutritional treatment is that the schizophrenic is spoiling his or her treatment by sneaking cokes, coffee, cigarettes, and so on, by not taking vitamins and medications correctly, or by not yet discovering and omitting key allergens in the air, water, and food.

How can the family help a schizophrenic with diet?

The family can help by going on the same basic diet prescribed for the schizophrenic.

This seems unnecessary. Why do you recommend that the *family* go on the diet?

First, the diet will not only certainly help other family members by the simple good health and nutrition it provides, but it will help keep offending foods, cigarettes, and beverages out of temptation's way for the schizophrenic.

Interestingly, and maybe vital since most forms of schizophrenia are inherited biochemical systems, at least one or two other family members probably have some of the same biochemical problems in lesser ways, so there may be dramatic changes for good health in those family members, too. Furthermore, brothers and sisters of the patient may also have inherited schizophrenia and not yet actually come down with symptoms of the disorder, so that many cases of schizophrenia in the future, may well be *prevented* by these simple nutritional measures.

7

Food allergies and sensitivities

What are food sensitivities?

In the early 1970s it was shown by Dr. F. C. Dohan that in-hospital schizophrenics who did not consume wheat and dairy products got better at roughly twice the rate of those who ate the usual hospital diet. The substances to which some schizophrenics may be sensitive in the wheat and milk have since been tentatively identified as complex protein molecules called "polypeptides." Polypeptides are able to penetrate into the brain—apparently more easily in some schizophrenics than non-schizophrenics. In the brain polypeptides are believed to act as toxic substances—worsening such schizophrenic symptoms as thought disorder, depression, fogginess, and sense of reality. The polypeptides in other cereal grain such as corn, rye, and barley may cause similar effects, but rice and oats are usually free of the toxic effects.

It now appears clear from many sources that there are actually three types of sensitivities to substances entering the body from air, water, skin, and food. While not all individual schizophrenics have these types of food sensitivities, they are *extremely* common. The first type of sensitivity is the well-known allergic "itching-'n-sneezing" type of reaction in which even very small amounts of a certain food or allergen such as dust or pollen in the environment cause a typical allergic reaction, such as hives, hayfever, or asthma.

What are the other two food sensitivities?

There is a second but much less known type, that seems to be a kind of food senstivity or intolerance. It is unlike classical allergy because the intensity of the reaction depends on how much food is eaten—that is, it is a "dose-related" sensitivity. So, if only small amounts of the offending substance are eaten at occasional intervals, there may be no reaction whatever, while eating lots of that food every day may cause substantial symptoms of various types. People with this type of food sensitivity often do not know they have it, because they eat these foods every day and chronically suffer these symptoms which they do not attribute to food. This is the type of food sensitivity that Dr. Dohan identified in his research.

Even less well known is the third type of food intolerance, which is a reaction similar to addiction to alcohol, caffeine, or heroin. These addictive reactions commonly occur to sugar, soft drinks, pastries, and so on—the well known "junk-food junkie" reaction—but they can occur with practically any food.

How do these food addictions work?

It is thought by some nutrition scientists, although much research needs to be done, that there may be something in the food which stimulates the endorphin addiction mechanisms in the brain.* So eating these addictive foods may be just like taking a shot of morphine! Many patients report a "high" just after eating these addictive foods with withdrawal symptoms a few hours later. Typical withdrawal symptoms are irritability, feelings of emptiness, craving, and depressive feelings (symptoms relieved by taking more of the offending food).

Do you mean patients react just as if they were addicted to alcohol or coffee?

Yes. A late-night ice box orgy produces typical morning hangover symptoms in susceptible persons. Patients and families should eliminate beverages, foods, cigarettes, etc., that the schizophrenic seems to be "hooked" on.

Isn't this food sensitivity problem too complicated for a confused schizophrenic just beginning treatment?

Really sticking to every item on the diet suggested in the past few pages can be very difficult. It takes time, persistence, and effort to learn all the ins and outs of these allergies and sensitivities and to follow them carefully.

In actual practice, then, in the early weeks and months of treatment, many schizophrenics living at home and in community residences find it difficult or psychologically impossible to give up everything at once—corn, wheat and milk products, sugar, tobacco, coffee, alcohol, and, in addition, food fads and addictions—to say nothing of finding out and omitting other specific foods to which they are allergic or sensitive.

It still sounds complicated!

Nothing to get upset about! The treatment of schizophrenia must be viewed by the patient and family as an attack on a whole series of influences which makes schizophrenia

*Endorphins are highly addictive morphine-like substances naturally secreted in the brain.

worse (poor nutritional habits, lack of exercise, excessive coffee and alcohol intake, doses of schizophrenia medications that are too high or too low, irregular daily habits, allergies and sensitivities, and inadequately treated medical conditions)—*anything* preventing the best body function.

At first it is not technically possible to do everything on the list—even Superman could not make all those changes overnight! So the whole idea is to attack the most important and easiest ones first and then as time, persistence, and effort permit, take the next problem on the list.

The whole idea in any long term treatment is to be patient, using trial and error, persistence, and cooperation with a knowledgeable psychiatrist/counselor/nutritionist combination with *much* dialogue with other schizophrenic families, such as through the local chapter of the National Alliance for the Mentally Ill.

What can be done to make it simpler at first?

For simplicity, it is suggested as a compromise that the schizophrenic *totally* avoid caffeine, alcohol, and marijuana, which are the usual worst offending substances, and also keep a diet low but not totally free of foods containing sugar, wheat, and milk—hence the maxim, "Eat a minimum of foods containing sugar, milk, and wheat." Schizophrenics should follow this maxim with the understanding that this is only the first step for a complete diet plan to be developed later. We believe that a huge majority of schizophrenics who follow the nutritional "dos and don'ts" we suggest will improve nicely on this regime and not gain excessive weight. One of the best features of nutritional therapy for schizophrenics is that it allows for much smaller doses of medication—or none at all—with consequent lessening of unpleasant side effects.

After the schizophrenia is under good control, what should the patient do?

At the appropriate time the schizophrenic and his or her

family should plan a convenient time to really do a complete, careful, meticulous trial of *absolutely no* wheat or milk products, corn or corn products, milk and milk products, and a minimum of sugar-containing foods, because this diet will usually further improve the well-being of a schizophrenic as well as magnificently manage any overweight problems! If the schizophrenic is still not doing well, an ecologically oriented allergist should be consulted. Naturally, schizophrenics having a *history* of allergies should see an allergist (the local National Alliance for the Mentally Ill will also have this name and telephone number) just as early as possible in treatment. The schizophrenia itself may not improve in this group until this treatment is instituted. In addition, schizophrenics who are simply not progressing well despite a reasonable effort on the "dos and don'ts" should make a beeline for the allergist or clinical ecologist because they are likely to have major offending food sensitivities or allergies to account for their failure to improve.

What clues suggest a possible food sensitivity or allergy?

There are several tell-tale signs: a stuffy nose accompanied by an open-mouthed, rather vague look due to the schizophrenic's necessity for mouth breathing. There may also be a puffy face, circles under the eyes, and difficulty paying attention. A schizophrenic often complains of chronic fatigue, even with plenty of sleep, but may also feel somewhat nervous and restless at the same time. Overweight schizophrenics should *always* be considered as possibly food and allergy sensitive until proven otherwise, as excessive fad or "addictive" eating tends to put on weight.

I notice our schizophrenic gets much better at times and worse at other times. What causes this?

That happens a lot. We really do not know the cause of

every change in mood and symptom. The cause of mood change, of course, may be found in how well the schizophrenic follows the "dos and don'ts." However, everyone's inner emotional feelings change with events in his lifetime—such as the pride and glow of beating the cigarette habit, falling in love, getting a first job, or losing the first twenty pounds. Also, plain and simple, it is exciting *just to feel better* and to understand that the symptoms of schizophrenia can be controlled by specific actions (such as omitting certain foods and jogging twenty minutes each day).

As a schizophrenic feels better he or she actually suffers less from his or her allergies—the sensitivity and allergic reactions actually lessen with general improvement in the schizophrenia, which then, in turn, makes the schizophrenic feel even better!

"I just can't give up cigarettes" or "I just can't give up coffee, junk foods, coke, etc."

Don't you believe it! Any of these habits can be given up. Schizophrenics at my office stop lifelong addictive habits all the time! *Whatever* the schizophrenic is hooked on, it is almost certainly making him feel worse, so he or she can count on feeling better after only a few days. By the end of three to seven days the compulsive addiction will ease up and the schizophrenic will already feel much better. It may take patience and effort, but it is vital to tackle each one of them, one after another, patiently and sensibly. It is *so* important to stop *every* addiction that the schizophrenic should do *anything*, including rehospitalization, to stop his habit. *Any* habit can be broken with will, persistence, and imagination no matter how "weak" a schizophrenic feels he or she is.

With improvement, of course, the ego, the inner strength of the individual, gets better so that everything gets increasingly easier with time. "If at first you don't succeed, try, try again!" If it is any consolation, it took the author six serious attempts before he totally got rid of a heavy cigarette habit.

8

Environment at home and at work

From what the book has said so far, it is clear that taking care of the body (good food and plenty of exercise) and paying attention to medications and allergic reactions are important. Surely family attitudes and behavior are important too?

Naturally, the family feeling and the atmosphere in the home are very important. One way to look at the family emotional atmosphere in which the schizophrenic lives is to see it from the same perspective as the allergic-toxic environment discussed earlier. That is, schizophrenics can thrive in a large variety of different family atmospheres so long as the "toxic" ones are avoided.

What is a "toxic" family atmosphere?

Generally, schizophrenics are not seriously bothered by tangible, practical family problems, such as financial difficulties or a relative's illness. Rather, they are most likely to become overwrought by two basic factors in the family atmosphere: constant negative feelings in the air—anger, resentment, guilt, cruelty, tension, anxiety, depression—and a hectic, noisy, raucous pace of daily living that is unsettling, overwhelming, and filled with tension and anxiety due to pressure. The incessant activity of even a normally busy home can be toxic if it does not allow for privacy and quiet, peaceful rest periods.

What happens to a schizophrenic in a toxic situation?

Let us say that the schizophrenic lives in a home in which a family member drinks too much. Whether the drinking causes a lot of arguments or a lot of quiet desperation, anxiety, and resentment beneath the surface, the schizophrenic will always be on edge and anxious over what might happen next.

Constant worry, guilt, tension, and fear act as stimulants to schizophrenics. These pressures make it difficult for them to relax during the day, to concentrate, to think clearly, and to sleep well at night. Actually, in these situations schizophrenics may seek temporary solace in starting to drink themselves. Of course, this drinking can only lead to a downhill, crisis-ridden course for both the schizophrenic and the family if it is not controlled. This pattern of overstimulation followed by drinking is one of the most common causes of schizophrenic relapse and rehospitalization.

Why don't the everyday problems bother the schizophrenic in the same way that toxic ones do?

The tension and anxiety associated with practical family problems usually do not last long enough to cause harm in the average family. When the family is working together at solving a financial or other problem, a closer relationship tends to develop among its members. Of course, there may be flare-ups, arguments, and tensions when families really get seriously worried, but the usual family "kisses and makes up" afterward, allowing any emotional wounds to heal. It is only the constant negative feelings that are toxic, hassling and gradually wearing down the schizophrenic to the point of relapse. Through its stimulant action, the never-healing, aggravating, emotional atmosphere of guilt, anxiety, depression, and tension causes the relapse.

What should the schizophrenic and family do if the atmosphere becomes toxic?

The first thing the family should *avoid* doing is sitting back and blaming each other for the situation. This only makes matters worse. If the family cannot banish these negative attitudes from the home through ordinary family conferences, then the family's schizophrenia counselor (discussed in depth in Chapter 13) should be consulted. If this proves impossible, the schizophrenic must find another place to live. If the problem seems to be solvable with time, the schizophrenic may choose to obtain an increased dose of medications from the doctor and wait out the situation. The schizophrenic must, however, with help from doctor and/or counselor, be able to determine whether the problem has been or can be solved. One of the most common reasons for rehospitalizations is repeatedly returning home from the hospital only to find the toxic family atmosphere unresolved. So, another rule is, *"Don't live in a toxic atmosphere."*

What can be done for mild toxic conditions when the schizophrenic does not want to move out?

In some cases, the schizophrenic or a family member behaves in such a manner as to be a constant toxic irritation within the family. In this case, family counseling is often helpful.

Suppose psychotherapy does not resolve the toxic situation and the schizophrenic is not employed?

One of the most underestimated aggravations in the schizophrenic's family is the tension that can build up when the passive schizophrenic just hangs around the house—too much in the way, too close, too involved with other family members. If the schizophrenic is still too sick to work, he or she may do best by going to a day care center of some type every day. One study in England clearly showed that schizophrenics who are away from home eight hours a day improve more rapidly than those who don't get out of the house. One of the best solutions to this problem is having the schizophrenic work at the house of a relative or neighbor, volunteer each day at a hospital, nursing home, farm, or similar place, until he or she is ready for paid part-time or full-time employment.

How does the mere presence of the schizophrenic produce a toxic atmosphere?

There is nothing worse for a schizophrenic of any age than just sitting or lying around all day while the wife, mother, husband—everyone else!—works. Family members come to resent the unfairness of having a lazy drone around. It bothers them that the schizophrenic is not getting anywhere and is not improving. It positively horrifies them to think that the disorder, with its lack of initiative and its inactivity, is not being resolved and may remain so indefinitely. Getting the schizophrenic going—somehow producing momentum toward recovery—is the essential solution to this problem.

Can other factors cause a toxic atmosphere?

A large number of factors can destroy the proper family

atmosphere. Depression in a family member can really trap the family in a bitter, resentful, guilty tension. Drug addictions, notably dependency on pills such as Valium and Librium, have the same negative effects on the family as excessive drinking. Another common problem in some families is the lack of a leader. These families simply don't know how to solve problems of any kind. They don't know how to take responsible action. The result is a chronic, vague chaos. No matter what anyone does or says, it causes trouble—and constant toxic, negative feelings.

Another important contribution to a toxic atmosphere in some families is a refusal or inability to accept schizophrenia for what it is. This problem has several ramifications. First, the families and patients may expect either too little or too much from the schizophrenic, which makes for frustrations, resentments, and too much or too little pressure for performance by the schizophrenic.

Occasionally some families may seem willing to settle for the schizophrenic in his ill state. These families may actually seem to prefer the schizophrenic to be ill, giving the family a purpose, a central focus, so they can feel useful in caring for the sick schizophrenic. This prevents the loneliness that some families fear would set in if the schizophrenic got well and left home. These types of families produce a cloying, resentful, overprotective tension that is toxic to the schizophrenic. Happily, these families are not common. However, they often absorb enormous amounts of professional time and may be written up. This tends to make some professionals regard them as typical cases when, in actuality, they are rare. Obviously, this produces false images of schizophrenia to the general public.

How does incessant activity in the family atmosphere cause toxic problems?

Some families have happy, active, busy lifestyles that are wonderful for nonschizophrenics but that may be toxic to some schizophrenics through the overstimulating effects.

Schizophrenics in this kind of household don't have sufficient opportunity to slow down and proceed at a comfortable pace. Usually, all that is necessary to resolve this situation is to make special arrangements for the schizophrenic to have the privacy he or she needs. This can mean merely assigning the schizophrenic a private room and setting a family rule that no one disturbs the schizophrenic when the door is closed.

What other family problems can cause trouble?

One troublesome situation—well publicized in the psychiatric literature because it is so difficult to deal with—is the presence of an extra-close bond between two family members. This occurs most frequently between mother and child; interestingly, it occurs much less often between schizophrenic and spouse. In any case, these two tend to isolate themselves from the rest of the family, and from society in general, for fear that any interest outside themselves—relationships with other people or involvement in a vocation, for example—will split them up. This type of mutually overprotective, exclusive relationship is called symbiosis. It is uncommon, but when it evolves, it narrows down opportunities for fun, social activities, vocational progress, and general personal development because neither of the two individuals can trust the other to go out and do things in the community. Characteristic of these people are a low opinion of themselves and the fear that the loved one will automatically prefer outsiders if allowed to make friends at all.

The importance of this problem results in two good general maxims for schizophrenics: *"Love more than one,"* and, *"Put your emotional eggs in more than one basket."*

What problems affect schizophrenics who live alone?

This depends on how schizophrenics manage their lives. If they work all day and are socially active on weekends, or if they live active but steady and comfortable retirement years, they may do just fine on their own. But if they spend a lot of time at home doing relatively little—daydreaming or living in a television-oriented fantasy land—thus lacking the action, interest, and involvement necessary to healthful living, relapse gradually occurs. It is interesting to note that many schizophrenics seem to get keyed up from boredom itself. In such cases, schizophrenics describe the feeling as a gradually building emotional pressure from within. These pressures often explode into preoccupations with meaningless rituals, various types of paranoid thinking, or even into fantasies of violence of one kind or another. As these symptoms worsen, the schizophrenic usually suffers from insomnia no matter how much time he or she spends in bed. In turn, the presence of insomnia only speeds up the relapse process.

Does this mean that most schizophrenics should not live alone?

Yes. It is not normal for anyone to be a hermit. Normal people fall prey to "cabin fever," with symptoms that resemble schizophrenia, when they live alone. They feel lonely when they lose the human contacts that give them a sense of family and community, which enriches, teaches, satisfies, and makes life meaningful. Active schizophrenics who live in a house or apartment alone are, on the other hand, not alone in the same sense as schizophrenics who are isolated within *themselves* at home. Therefore, with notable exceptions, another maxim for schizophrenics is, *"Do not live alone."*

Do all these causes of toxic atmosphere apply to the schizophrenic's work atmosphere?

Yes. Working in a toxic environment does "do a job" on the schizophrenic in the same way that toxic living at home does. Of course, schizophrenics spend less time at work and usually are less intensely and emotionally involved in work than in family, so conditions that are intolerable at home can often be shrugged off at work. One problem facing the working schizophrenic is that certain jobs tend to produce such a fast pace that continues long enough to prevent the schizophrenic from calming down in the evening. As a result, the schizophrenic is continually in toxic surroundings with all their consequent overstimulation.

Can the schizophrenic's job cause any other significant problems?

The fact that schizophrenics tend to be supersensitive, to worry excessively about those around them, or to dread the consequences of making mistakes can cause on-the-job problems. Schizophrenics who find themselves in some kind of leadership position often get keyed up by the pressure of their responsibilities. If this occurs, the intelligent schizophrenic will often do well to take a less worrisome type of job.

Should a schizophrenic work at night?

No! Even though night jobs are often easier to find, working at night somehow disturbs the schizophrenic's normal circadian sleep-wake cycle so that sleep is not satisfying.

An emotional problem for married schizophrenics and those who live with close-knit families is that working during weekends, nights, and holidays may make them miss essential family activities—the times when emotionally nutrient, loving, exciting togetherness takes place. When both schizophrenic and spouse are working, one of them working during nights, weekends, or holidays may prevent them from seeing each other enough to maintain a happy, comfortable marriage.

"Schizophrenics usually should not work at night, on weekends, or on holidays."

9

Rehabilitation and passivity

What is the difference between rehabilitation and treatment?

In the public mind, *treatment* of any disorder usually involves management of the patient through administration of some medication or through some physical procedure such as surgery or physiotherapy. On the other hand, *rehabilitation* usually refers to a gradual restoration of the patient to his or her former condition, which implies long-term therapy and a chronic condition.

As used in this book, rehabilitation means something much broader than simple medical treatment. It usually refers to two to three years in which the patient is motivated and activated, learns good health skills, resumes vocational and academic activities, and returns to normal social and recreational living.

What is the greatest obstacle to successful rehabilitation?

Besides the patient's and family's difficulties in fully accepting the schizophrenia as a disorder in itself, probably the single most difficult problem in the rehabilitation of the schizophrenic is passivity. To repeat, schizophrenia is a disease of initiative. Many, if not most, schizophrenics lose their general sense of motivation, energetic enthusiasm, and executive capabilities. They often just do nothing when a problem presents itself, helplessly and childishly turning to someone else to solve the problem when they could easily handle it themselves.

How is this passivity treated?

Action is the keynote. Family members must use any method—firmness, pushing, cajoling, persuading—to get the schizophrenic moving. A combination of physical activity, exercise, and active social groups is the best approach to start with.

Why is exercise important?

Exercise is important for physical and mental health because it keeps muscles strong, increases circulation, and maintains the hundreds of biochemical systems in the body. Good exercise *feels* better. However, exercise does much more for schizophrenics; it keeps them alive and aware. It is easy to tell whether schizophrenics have been generally physically active because they tend to be more alert, more lively and sharp, if they have been exercising. If they have been sitting around doing nothing, they tend to be inactive and lethargic the next day. Vigorous physical activity also seems to activate those parts of the brain that are involved with interest, motivation, initiative, and purposeful action.

Doesn't exercise stimulate an already overstimulated brain?

Actually it doesn't work that way in this case. At this point it is important to understand the cause of the passivity that is so difficult to treat once it is established. In a sense, the schizophrenic brain has more emotional "steam pressure" than it can handle. This emotional pressure is extremely uncomfortable, making the schizophrenic feel tense, anxious, and frightened, and possibly triggering some of the schizophrenic symptoms. Because of this discomfort, most schizophrenics quickly learn to tone down this overactivity by avoiding too many upsetting stimuli. They do this by being quiet and passive. Exercise then reverses the unfortunate tendency of the schizophrenic to slow down at the very time that activity is called for to make them feel better. At the same time, exercise vents the emotional pressures that have built up. As a result, exercise and physical activity, in a sense, function as tranquilizers through their energizing effects.

"Schizophrenics should get plenty of moderate exercise every day."

So exercise and physical activity make the schizophrenic more normal?

Absolutely. When the schizophrenic's excess reactivity is calmed down, he can now take more environmental pressure. He or she can stand more upsetting events in life. A schizophrenic can enter more into the natural, normal pressures of everyday living—which then make these activities more *interesting* rather than upsetting—because the pressures no longer cause the schizophrenic to build up so much uncomfortable emotional steam. (*See* Bibliography.)

But don't all people "burn off" energy in this way?

Certainly. Many schizophrenics and most nonschizophrenics do learn to manage emotional pressure by using a balance of *both* exercise and physical activity and regular rest. However, it is characteristic of the schizophrenic illness to gradually evolve into a passive, quiet lifestyle with relatively much less interest, motivation, and initiative.

Why is exercise especially important for the passive schizophrenic?

A schizophrenic who regresses to a severe passive, "do nothing" state is in a dreadful vicious cycle of "*the more stimulated he is the more he needs to quiet down by avoiding further stimulating events.*" This, in turn, causes more emotional pressure. It becomes literally a lifesaving matter for the schizophrenic to relieve his emotional pressure by becoming physically active, because his inactivity becomes a difficult-to-break habit that further regresses him to a dismal mental state. Families should not be reluctant to be very firm in their insistence that the schizophrenic exercise daily. I recommend jogging 20 minutes a day without stopping.

Why is it so difficult to break the passive-inactive lifestyle habits?

Inactive people, schizophrenic or nonschizophrenic, who do not take initiative or act on their natural curiosity just don't get as involved in life or as interested in doing things as they should. When people are not interested in things, they don't learn how to do them. They don't learn how to dance, row a boat, talk to the opposite sex, or cook. Without these skills they develop no self-confidence. Without confidence, it is difficult to proceed to action—another vicious cycle of passivity.

In addition, quiet, passive, or inactive people are not actively loving. They tend to wait for others to come to them with love. This lack of initiative toward others tends to hurt the others' feelings, which only causes them to be less loving. This in turn makes the inactive person feel even less loved and less confident—another vicious cycle!

One more serious result of this passive process is embarrassment. The schizophrenic is afraid of being laughed at and looking foolish for making mistakes. This, of course, is made worse by the lack of skills and confidence the inactive person feels. Unfortunately, this self-consciousness throws the true situation out of proportion, forcing schizophrenics to believe they are far more incompetent than they actually are.

For all these reasons, the inactive, passive schizophrenic finds it exceedingly difficult to break the passive lifestyle. Therefore, the rehabilitation must confront this problem when it appears.

Why is it so important for the family to understand the schizophrenic's inactivity and passivity?

The schizophrenic's rehabilitation is totally dependent on everyone involved understanding exactly how shy, frightened, and unconfident the schizophrenic really is inside, no matter what the surface appearance. Otherwise, the aggravation and exasperation brought on by this passivity is likely to turn into complete intolerance of the patient's apparent stubbornness in refusing to make efforts to help himself.

How is this understanding needed in rehabilitation?

Rehabilitation for the schizophrenic is similar to rehabilitation for the victim of any disorder. It consists of returning the patient to normal functioning. When the schizophrenic illness puts the schizophrenic out of commission for a while, self-confidence is lost. Schizophrenics commonly fear that trying again will only return them to the normal life in which they failed before, bringing back the extremely unpleasant, tense, desperate, emotionally steam-pressured life they were attempting to escape by becoming quiet, passive, and isolated. They are afraid of getting "burned" again by returning to a life which made them sick in the first place. Even when schizophrenics are assured that their medications will relieve fears and tensions, and when they have actually experienced this relief, they remain naturally reluctant to renew their normal lives. Having recently been so horribly sick and miserable leaves the schizophrenic with an intense fear of a recurrence. When the schizophrenic and family understand these feelings, they can prevent much of the anger, exasperation, and discouragement that are toxic to the schizophrenic who is struggling back to normal living. Schizophrenics and their families will be rewarded by the patient's ability to handle situations without reacting with unpleasant tensions once serious rehabilitation has begun.

What happens when the schizophrenic wants to get well but is also afraid to get well?

When schizophrenics notice their first real progress, they often react with limited enthusiasm because they are afraid that these early successes won't last. Sometimes the schizophrenic even tends to avoid the enthusiasm itself, because it is a kind of stimulating emotion that often leads to familiar fear, tension, and desperation, just as it did in the past. With continued progress, the schizophrenic begins to trust the rehabilitation process and becomes generally more active and confident. This process is called "rehabilitation momentum."

How does rehabilitation momentum work?

Rehabilitation momentum reverses the vicious cycle of inactivity and lack of confidence, replacing it with an action-oriented series of enthusiastic successes, which in turn make for more enthusiasm and greater effort. Possibly the single most important skill in the schizophrenic's rehabilitation is that developed by the schizophrenic, counselor, and family to maintain enthusiastic but calm participation until the schizophrenic can comfortably find a niche in the everyday world of nonschizophrenics.

What about schizophrenics who are not passive-inactive?

Rehabilitation is much easier for those who are not passive-inactive because they can get moving with fewer problems. However, all schizophrenics are quite shaken by the devastating effects of the illness itself, and they fear to return to it once they feel better. So, lack of confidence and motivation are problems experienced to some degree by those with any form of schizophrenia. In fact, these problems crop up during rehabilitation of any disorder.

Schizophrenics must face the embarrassment of social stigma problems, their fear of relapse, the upset family situation, and so on, and they must do all this at first with incomplete alertness and functioning capacity to think, evaluate, and solve problems. So it is difficult for every schizophrenic to try to return to normal living even if the schizophrenic is not handicapped by the passive-inactive problem.

What about the schizophrenic who really doesn't think normal living is worth regaining?

Schizophrenics who had unhappy childhoods and consequent personality problems, as well as those currently living in unhappy, unpleasant situations, are less highly motivated to return to reality than are those schizophrenics who are feeling intense mental suffering but live in a loving, sensible environment. The more they suffer from the disorder, the more likely schizophrenics are to try to get better; having a pleasant environment to return to only increases the motivation. For these reasons, the rehabilitation team must understand the total effort the schizophrenic can make at first, and the basic reasons for the individual's degree of motivational intensity, so that the rehabilitation team can pace its efforts effectively for each individual.

What is the rehabilitation team?

The rehabilitation team includes all those who participate in the schizophrenic's recovery—counselor, family, school, vocational personnel, and others. Nothing less than an active team effort will be enough to rehabilitate the more seriously ill schizophrenic. Schizophrenics whose illness is less serious often need no more than the basic medical team because after improving medically, they are able to gather and maintain their own momentum of recovery.

Is it common for schizophrenics to suffer less serious cases of the illness?

Yes. These schizophrenics are much less well-known by rehabilitation people because they are not seen as often in mental hospitals nor studied as much by psychiatrists since they tend to recover rapidly on their own. In fact, the less seriously ill are a basically active group of schizophrenics quite common in "medical" psychiatrists' offices. Unfortunately, the public's conception, developed through the writings of psychiatrists, is that mild cases of schizophrenia do not occur or are uncommon. Nothing could be farther from the truth.

Do the same principles of rehabilitation apply to the treatment of mild cases of the various types of schizophrenia?

Yes; the only difference is in the amount of effort required. Complicating the problem of public awareness is the fact that, as indicated earlier, the mildest cases of schizophrenia have often been called acute schizophrenia, paraphenia, cyclothymic schizophrenia, and even certain types of manic-depressive illness. A trend has developed to reserve the use of the word *schizophrenia* for only the process and paranoid types.

Has this new trend become a problem in rehabilitation?

Although it generally has had a good effect in differentiating apparently different disorders, this trend has also caused further confusion in diagnoses. Because no specific reliable laboratory tests for each type of schizophrenia are yet available, these new names are often incorrectly used in actual clinical practice to designate patients who have only mild cases of paranoid or process schizophrenia. As a result, the medical management and rehabilitation treatment that is so important may often be inappropriate or delayed until the diagnosis is clear. This is just another reason why an accurate early diagnosis is so important to the rehabilitation of schizophrenia.

How much difference will this problem of terminology make?

On one hand, as long as the rehabilitation process is sound, the name of the disorder clearly is inconsequential. On the other hand, in some cases the medications themselves and many of the specific rehabilitative techniques will differ or be confused if the type of schizophrenia is inaccurately named or not named at all. *Even in this book, the term* schizophrenia *is applied to any persistent thinking disorder that does not have some other known medical cause, such as fever, brain tumor, or thyroid condition.* As clinical experiences are collected and diagnosis, medical treatment, and rehabilitation are further refined, even further specific clarity will be needed in the treatment of each disorder.

10

Mini-relapses

What do you term a mini-relapse?

A mini-relapse is a worsening of schizophrenic symptoms without a full return to schizophrenic illness. There is no such thing as a completely smooth recovery from schizophrenia or from any other disorder. In the course of rehabilitation, the patient will always encounter hills and valleys, plateaus, regressions, crises, and triumphs. A mini-relapse usually indicates that the rehabilitation is not going well or that some significant stress is weighing on the schizophrenic. A mini-relapse is extremely useful as an early warning of a complete relapse that may follow days or weeks later. This allows plenty of time to alert the schizophrenic and family that changes in lifestyle or home situation should be made to prevent a relapse and to maintain the momentum of rehabilitation.

What causes mini-relapses?

By far the most common cause of mini-relapses in schizophrenia is violation of the dos and don'ts discussed earlier, especially those concerning the use of alcohol and coffee, and those dealing with sleep habits. Sometimes, however, there are less obvious causes. When the schizophrenic returns to college or loses a close friend, or when the family has an argument, the schizophrenic may tend to isolate himself and feel an increase in fear, tension, suspiciousness, self-consciousness, or difficulty in concentration. He or she may experience peculiar sensations or a sense of detachment.

Aren't these types of stress normal and unavoidable?

Yes. Young adults do go to college and most families do argue now and then, and all those involved will show signs of strain. Like normal people, schizophrenics cannot face a major social event without some fear and tension. Average stresses and strains like these seldom result in a mini-relapse. *Mini-relapses usually occur only when stresses and strains are continuous and unresolved, or when the schizophrenic is not yet ready to take on a new responsibility.* Sometimes the continuous strain of a new job, for instance, may last for several weeks, and some schizophrenic symptoms may temporarily return while the schizophrenic masters the new job.

How can the patient and family distinguish the true mini-relapse from the normal and natural stresses of life?

A simple check of all the dos and don'ts with the schizophrenic usually will indicate whether or not the problem is due to poor habits. When the problem is clearly not a violation of one of the dos and don'ts, then the source of the stress usually can be pinpointed quickly because it is almost always a matter that is on the minds of the schizophrenic and family. That is, everybody is concerned with the specific event that is the basic problem—the family argument, the schizophrenic's fear and worry about returning to high school in the fall, or the schizophrenic's fear of not being accepted by coworkers upon returning to a job following a schizophrenic episode. Generally, when schizophrenic symptoms reappear, signaling a mini-relapse, if there has been no violation of the dos and don'ts, the situation is temporary and self-limited. If the symptoms do not disappear soon, prompt action must be taken.

What action should the family take?

The first thing to do is to make a special effort to determine whether the schizophrenic is trying too much, pushing himself too hard, or is being pushed too hard by others. The second move is to make a special urgent appointment with the counselor or psychiatrist to try to identify other problems—medication reactions, physical disease, patient "cheating" on the dos and don'ts, or hidden toxic family or social problems. Because schizophrenics seldom "go crazy" overnight unless drugs are involved, watching for early signs of mini-relapse usually prevents the major relapse, as long as the schizophrenic is willing to follow the dos and don'ts. Schizophrenics who follow the dos and don'ts reasonably well rarely relapse to the point of rehospitalization unless there is some problem with medications.

How do the schizophrenic and family judge the progress of rehabilitation?

Family and patient must understand what these mini-relapse symptoms really mean, lest they become discouraged or frightened about the schizophrenic's progress. Mini-relapse symptoms are excellent indicators of the general progress of rehabilitation. Normally, schizophrenic symptoms will gradually improve during the rehabilitation period. However, when the schizophrenic jumps to some new responsibility, takes on more working hours, or has to face extra social events during the course of recovery, the symptoms may temporarily worsen, which is merely a sign that the patient is tackling these fears and tensions. With success these symptoms will lessen in severity within a week or two, usually within a day or two. On the other hand, if the pressure is too strong, symptoms will continue and the schizophrenic will need to back off from whatever he or she is attempting and try it again more slowly. The schizophrenic and family must not fear these pressures and strains; they are natural and necessary as the schizophrenia improves. It is only when these strains and stresses continue that a slower pace of improvement may be required.

What else can cause schizophrenic symptoms to worsen?

The internal pressures of normal maturing can cause symptoms to reappear or worsen. Schizophrenics may feel extremely strained when they resume their responsibilities following the low period during which they were patients and were taken care of by others. They may not show much change in behavior on the surface, but inside they may be taking an important, emotionally stressful step in their lives. Everyone in the family can see that this is progress because it always follows a period of increasing maturity and improvement in the schizophrenic illness. Again, symptoms stemming from this internal stress usually subside within a few days because this is simply a response to normal life stress. Reactions to normal life stresses should not be feared because they are part of normal living and the symptoms will generally go away after a brief period of time. On the other hand, when a mini-relapse is brought on by the schizophrenic's playing games with coffee and alcohol, he or she usually has taken a step backward in maturity and acts or looks more childish, more mischievous, and more immature—behavior that is readily recognizable to both patient and family. The schizophrenic who is making mature progress, even though his symptoms are slightly worsening, exhibits an aura of seriousness, earnestness, and dignity. This contrasts with the erratic, immature, childish, or cocky behavior of the schizophrenic who is having a mini-relapse that precedes a major relapse of the schizophrenic illness.

11

Typical family problems

In general, of course, schizophrenics have the same family problems that nonschizophrenics have—personality problems, behavior problems, physical illnesses, financial problems, school problems, and jealousy. However, one specific problem that affects families with handicaps is their efforts to hide their toxic negative feelings. Families must make many accommodations when they have to learn to live with handicaps such as arthritis, asthma, and schizophrenia. Sometimes they are prevented from, say, going to the circus, entertaining, or participating in other normal activities by the limitations of the illness. Consequently, extra burdens, disappointments, and resentments face these families. In addition, unless thoroughly familiar with exactly how to treat the handicap, families tend to "walk on eggshells" out of fear of causing a relapse by doing or saying the wrong thing or by expressing resentments that will upset the patient. Schizophrenic families who do not know how to handle the schizophrenic may be too easy to please, overprotective, and overconcerned with the schizophrenic, which creates the unhappy illusion that the schizophrenic is more immature, handicapped, and sicker than he or she is.

How does the schizophrenic react to this attitude?

The schizophrenic reacts by *acting* more handicapped, more immature, and more ill. Like other family members, schizophrenics tend to respond with what is expected, acting the way they are treated. This problem is complicated by fear-driven efforts of the schizophrenic and family to avoid the pressures they think made the schizophrenic sick in the first place. With the best of intentions, they try to hide their negative feelings rather than resolve them.

What problems does this "hiding" technique create?

The major problem in this type of situation is that nobody in the family really succeeds in hiding anything from anybody. Certainly the schizophrenic is never fooled either. What really happens, unfortunately, is that the family actually produces a toxic family atmosphere through unsuccessful attempts to hide these resentments, fears, and guilts, plus the usual babying and overprotection. Thus the schizophrenic ends up feeling like a burden, a source of anxiety, a bother, and a disappointment to the family.

What can the family and schizophrenic do about this problem?

Since schizophrenics cannot be deceived about these tensions and fears, the family must hold a candid discussion of them now and then to clear the air. This is where family schizophrenia counselors may serve their most important function—to help identify, discuss, and resolve any fears, resentments, or tensions that arise. While nonschizophrenic families can often hide negative feelings with relatively little risk, schizophrenics who are supersensitive or "allergic" to these feelings cannot tolerate constantly concealed negative feelings. Schizophrenics thrive best in a family environment that is basically contented. Contentment is not obtained by avoiding problems; it is created by coming up with family solutions to them.

What else should the family watch for?

People play games like checkers or Monopoly for the excitement of competition, venting various feelings and having fun with each other in a harmless way. Game playing in the family serves the same purposes, except the basic pleasure, the "payoff," lies in getting revenge on the other person. Some schizophrenics are especially prone to playing these hurtful games because they are so deprived of the usual gratifications and pleasures of life, such as feeling loved, taking pride in achievement, feeling as if they "belong," and succeeding in competition, that they must resort to less satisfying pleasures. They take revenge on others through the process of watching them become helplessly irritated, angry, and frustrated.

The following scenario is just one example of the type of game a schizophrenic might play. Wife says, "Please empty the wastebasket into the trash barrel." Schizophrenic husband replies, "I don't want to because it will make me sick." Wife, resentful but "walking on eggshells" because she is afraid to upset the schizophrenic, then says, "Oh, I'm sorry; I'll do it myself." At this point the schizophrenic knows that he has won the "game of laziness" by avoiding his chores and also by upsetting his wife, thereby achieving the dubious pleasure of "getting her goat."

Of course, the schizophrenic actually loses because the pleasure of hurting his wife makes her resentful and thus creates a toxic emotional atmosphere for himself, which only worsens his schizophrenia. Hundreds of these get-sick self-defeating games can be played within the family circle to the detriment of both the schizophrenic and the family.

How can the family spot a schizophrenic game?

This is easier than it might sound. The schizophrenic always wears a secretive not-very-funny smile during the proceedings. This smile bursts into a kind of hollow laughter when the schizophrenic is challenged by direct questions such as, "Why are you smiling?" or "What are you smiling about?" The schizophrenic always knows that this is part of the game—the louder he or she denies it, the more likely it is to be true.

How does one distinguish this from normal teasing within a family?

The aim of normal teasing is not to hurt someone, but to produce a tender feeling. The schizophrenic game produces hurt feelings, embarrassment, or resentment and is harmful to the schizophrenic and family.

What makes up the proper atmosphere for the schizophrenic and family?

Good relationships produce good feelings. The best atmosphere for rehabilitation of schizophrenia is an honest, forthright, earnest, clear relationship between the family and the schizophrenic. It should be free of deception, lies, trickery, and hostility. The natural resentments that arise when two or more people live together should be talked out and resolved by sincere apologies when necessary and by "kissing and making up."

In addition, the occurrence of schizophrenic games always signals a lack of active pleasure, active fun, and active gratification for the patient. For that reason, a lively, happy recreational life, both within and outside the family, in social and athletic relationships, is absolutely vital for the recovering schizophrenic.

Is it more beneficial for schizophrenics to live with their families than by themselves?

There is much confusion and disagreement among professionals on this matter. Some families seem to assume that the schizophrenic is too ill to leave. Other families, as well as some modern-day counselors, assume that the schizophrenic is usually better off away from the family and should be encouraged to leave. The truth is that when someone is very ill, regardless of the disorder, he or she needs a caring, even protective, environment. Patients receive the most protective care at first in the hospital; then, as they get better, they go home. While they are actively sick, they stop maturing, but as they recover, they start maturing again. Schizophrenics should stay at home until they are mature enough to leave the family. Like normal adolescents, they can successfully leave home only when they feel ready.

Schizophrenics who were already independent when the illness struck probably will have to wait before regaining that status. In summary, no hard and fast rules determine when the schizophrenic should leave the family unless the family atmosphere is toxic. Everything depends on the state of the schizophrenic's maturity and the individual wishes and needs of the schizophrenic and family.

What actually happens when schizophrenia strikes a married person?

Fortunately, when schizophrenia first comes on after marriage, the schizophrenia is usually less severe and the schizophrenic is adequately mature to carry on the marriage. In these marriages, separation and divorce are not commonly caused by the schizophrenia itself. When separation and divorce do occur, the same basic causes of separation and divorce as in nonschizophrenic marriages—incompatible personalities, sexual problems, economic problems, difficulties in disciplining the children, infidelity, and so on—come into play and are not basically related to the schizophrenia. The vast majority of marriages in which schizophrenia occurs do not end in divorce.

How do the schizophrenic and family know how mature the schizophrenic has become?

All the family has to do is ask the schizophrenic whether or not he or she honestly feels confident about leaving the family and taking up an independent life. By the time the schizophrenic is ready to leave, he or she will have practically no schizophrenic symptoms, will be able to make independent decisions without resentment, will be able to make and keep social friends, and will be bored at home. That is, although he or she might feel somewhat resentful at being babied and rebellious of family members' ways, the schizophrenic will be happily excited and, of course, a little scared at the prospect of going out into the world alone. Until that time, if the family atmosphere is adequate, the schizophrenic should go about the business of growing and living at home.

What happens when the schizophrenic feels an intense need to escape from the family?

An intense need to escape usually indicates a toxic family atmosphere, which makes the schizophrenic feel tense, nervous, and anxious. When the toxic atmosphere is enough to interfere with the rehabilitation process or threatens to cause a relapse, the schizophrenic should move out, but only to another family or a substitute family such as a halfway house or some other community residence. When he or she has sufficiently matured in this new "family," the schizophrenic should leave.

What is the difference between independence and escape?

The schizophrenic and family should not confuse the schizophrenic's need to escape—in the name of isolation or from a feeling of being crowded by an overprotective family—with the positive feeling that surrounds the schizophrenic's departure for a more interesting independent life elsewhere. True independence comes from maturing, not from forced separation or escape. The schizophrenic, family, and schizophrenia counselor who sense a desperate need for the schizophrenic to escape or separate, should look to resolve cloying, too-close relationships or other toxic family feelings, rather than try to force the schizophrenic to leave home or to stay.

Suppose the schizophrenia is just too severe for total independence for the schizophrenic?

Unhappily, there are really difficult problems like this, though they are not common. Sometimes the only real solution within the family is simply to accept the fact that much more progress is not possible and that the family must learn to live as contentedly as possible with the status quo. That is, the family has to accept that it has a chronic moderate handicap. Families that include paraplegics, arthritics, and the senile elderly do not have to be unhappy with this situation once they have accepted it. Acceptance is a very good solution to many otherwise impossible problems and must always come before all the alternatives can be worked out and met. The final adaptation—the final adjustment to the problem—can come only after the problem has been clearly identified and accepted, and the family has learned to live with it in a positive way.

The Serenity Prayer can be a big help to these families: "God grant me the serenity to accept the things I cannot change, the courage to change the things I can, and the wisdom to know the difference." Often, the schizophrenic and family decide that the schizophrenic will be happier in a community residence, living with a relative or another family, or in some similar solution. Ingenious solutions such as communes or religious communities sometimes provide a happy atmosphere.

What other family problems can affect the schizophrenic's progress?

Schizophrenics can have other handicaps such as depression, blindness, seizures, and mental retardation. Some families have several handicaps, making everything more difficult. One of the most difficult situations is that in which a spouse or parent is also handicapped. As discussed earlier, schizophrenics who have personality problems stemming from unhappy childhoods have special handicaps that complicate the schizophrenia. Another handicap—possibly the most difficult of all for schizophrenics—is a lack of honesty, which prevents them from facing and solving their many problems. In addition, schizophrenics who are addicted to alcohol, coffee, marijuana, or other drugs have serious handicaps besides their schizophrenia. These problems help to form a toxic family atmosphere in just about every instance. Most schizophrenics with this type of problem must undergo retraining-in-residence of sufficient structure and efficacy for them to gain some integrity. Tragically, many schizophrenics end up in real life-and-death encounters due to their drug and alcohol problems or from isolation from the community that rejects their intolerable behavior. In a very real sense, a dishonest or addicted schizophrenic, like a severely afflicted diabetic, lives in a continual medical emergency because the schizophrenia itself may receive inadequate medical care.

What can the family do about the most seriously handicapped schizophrenic?

The truth is that some schizophrenics cannot be treated

successfully because there is no effective treatment available or because the patient refuses treatment. While this is rare, when it does happen the most important step for the family to take is to accept that fact; i.e., that there is nothing they can do; that they are powerless, at least for now, to help the schizophrenic. (Of course, in the future, treatment may become available or the schizophrenic may change his or her mind and accept treatment.)

Having recognized that they have done their best, the family must now learn to let the schizophrenic go—to detach themselves from the patient. This detachment, which is the most responsible thing they can accomplish, consists of accepting the natural flow of events—whatever may happen—and accepting all circumstances, or "God's will," so to speak. The alternative is disaster; keeping a lifeline attached to the schizophrenic in the vain hope of rescue only delays the onset of severe emotional pain, like an alcoholic who is reaching the "bottom," which may eventually cause the schizophrenic to seek out help some time in the future.

The overprotective family tends to exhaust itself in irrelevant and sometimes self-defeating efforts, but the responsible family will maintain its own good health and sanity while waiting for a new treatment or for the schizophrenic to change his or her mind. Thus, the family is healthy and open to any new opportunity that presents itself.

12

Rehabilitation

What practical course should the schizophrenic follow upon returning home?

As soon as schizophrenics begin their rehabilitation, they should be careful to follow the dos and don'ts. The schizophrenic and family will see the counselor and/or psychiatrist regularly to monitor the patient's progress and medications. As the schizophrenia improves (and it will!) the schizophrenic follows a sequence of gradually increasing activity to return to normal living.

All schizophrenics with mild disorders will want to take off a week or two after returning from the hospital and before going back to work or school. Then, like anyone who has had a major illness, the schizophrenic probably will feel like becoming more active.

Those schizophrenics with more severe disorders will have to proceed more slowly. After a week or two of relaxing, they usually will start making themselves useful around the house doing routine outdoor and indoor jobs such as mowing the lawn, washing the dishes, running errands, cleaning windows, and so on. This is gradually followed by a return to full-time function. Depending on the seriousness of the illness and other factors, this process may take a week to six months or more.

In principle this is a relatively simple rehabilitation process. And in practice, many schizophrenics do return to full-time work in a matter of a few weeks. Others, however, need much more time and a much greater effort. It is a fact that most cases of schizophrenia are easy to rehabilitate through these simple measures. The only reason this fact is not better known is that solid rehabilitation techniques for treating schizophrenia in the home and community are fairly new.

What about the more severe, complicated, or chronic cases? Do they really improve?

Absolutely. These people require more time, more effort, more practice, and more thorough knowledge to get better. For instance, schizophrenics (and families) who have relapsed four or five times will display a whole set of defeatist attitudes because their efforts have failed so completely in the past. They may not be willing to put heart and soul into another attempt because they don't expect success. The first rehabilitation effort in these cases must be directed toward persuading them to try again—and to do it right this time. The family and counselor repeatedly must face and help resolve family situations summed up by comments such as these: "My husband [wife] really doesn't seem to want to try"; "We already tried that!"; or "We just couldn't seem to get him [her] busy at home."

One of the most important statements about schizophrenia rehabilitation that can be made is the following: *"Usually schizophrenics who don't want to do things or don't want to get going are simply too sick with confusion, poor concentration, and lack of confidence."* (Of course, the schizophrenic may be playing "games"—but the telltale smile will reveal this.)

When medication dosage seems to be correct, the main task for the schizophrenic and family is to learn and practice the dos and don'ts. Recovering schizophrenics who carefully follow the dos and don'ts gradually find themselves wanting to do more and feeling motivated to get busy at an easygoing pace. So, patience and understanding on everyone's part is essential. There is nothing difficult in the rehabilitation of even very ill patients. Success is mainly based on persistence, hard work, learning to handle setbacks, and absolutely meticulous management of the dos and don'ts.

What obstacles will the patient and family encounter?

Many schizophrenics and families go to incredible lengths to practice all but one or two of the dos and don'ts. For instance, the family may ignore the fact that Dad is drinking too much or that Mom keeps saying, "Well, just one or two cups of coffee or tea won't hurt her [the schizophrenic]." Sometimes brothers and sisters will be so noisy and intrusive that a toxic atmosphere develops in the home. When the spouse is away from home all the time, the schizophrenic may not get the support he or she needs—another problem that can create toxic conditions. Akinesia, a side effect of medications, occasionally strikes the schizophrenic, inducing a passive reaction almost identical to the passivity of schizophrenia itself. If the patient and family religiously follow the dos and don'ts and the schizophrenic remains unmotivated, akinesia is probably present.

Besides following the dos and don'ts, what active steps can the family take to help the schizophrenic progress?

One family member, spouse or parent, should take the

daily responsibility to *write down a list of activities expected of the schizophrenic during that day.* For some reason, just telling the schizophrenic to do something doesn't seem to work nearly as well as giving him or her a written list. (This is an extremely important observation made years ago by rehabilitation specialists.) At first, these lists should contain one or two hours of genuinely useful work around the house. Take care to avoid assigning "busy work," because it will only hurt the schizophrenic's feelings to find out that his work really wasn't useful! Action is the best therapy, and the family should make the schizophrenic a useful part of the household right from the beginning. This list should also include scheduled social activities, doctors' appointments, and so on. Activities should start in the morning at a scheduled time to help the schizophrenic get out of bed, something that is often a problem in beginning rehabilitation. Altogether, the schizophrenic should be kept steadily and comfortably busy throughout the day but with frequent rest periods at first.

Doesn't the schizophrenic resent being told what to do?

Usually, this is not a great problem. In fact, even the most competent, secure schizophrenics appreciate being helped to get started at first, though they may argue or complain for a while. Their concentration, energy, and confidence are at an all-time low so that helping them structure their day is, in fact, surprisingly well received.

Suppose the schizophrenic still balks?

Still on the mind of most schizophrenics is the fear of returning to the very life from which they retreated in the first place. They well remember those painful tensions and fears, the nightmare of the "emotional steam pressures" of their previous life, so they may be reluctant, even terrified, to start on the road to recovery. The schizophrenic will need reassurance from counselor and family that the rehabilitation will be gradual and easygoing enough to prevent such problems and that the medications and following the dos and dont's will prevent the feared relapse this time around.

Suppose the schizophrenic *still* doesn't budge?

Even though they realize the schizophrenic is afraid and confused at this time, the counselor and family nonetheless may need to be very firm in their insistence that the schizophrenic put forth effective effort. This is done simply by sitting the person down at home and in family sessions with the counselor to lay down the law—remembering to include a large measure of reassurance. For some reason, an intense session with the counselor and family—each confirming what the other says—seems to budge every schizophrenic who is following the dos and don'ts (unless akinesia or some unrecognized toxic effect comes into play).

Suppose the schizophrenic plays the "you-can't-make-me-do-it" game?

In some instances the schizophrenic who has been overprotected or who is severely institutionalized and has not been useful for months or years will play this lazy game so that he or she budges very slowly, if at all. The skilled family and counselor *together* can usually beat this through repeated serious group talks. The family has to prove that its old, overprotective, soft, spoiling attitudes are gone for good, that it really has formed a firm set of expectations for the schizophrenic. Any family that "means business" must, of course, consider reinstitutionalizing the schizophrenic—not as a penalty but to activate the patient. In fact, it is the actual process of teaching the schizophrenic to set tough, realistic expectations for himself that is so useful in instilling hope in the midst of the inner morass of fear, confusion, and inferiority. This loving toughness is the key to rehabilitation for all types of handicaps because in most cases it is absolutely necessary to touch the inner core of hopelessness with a firm helping hand. Reinstitutionalization is not necessary when the family and counselor are serious because the schizophrenic will sense this attitude and begin to believe, as they do, their absolute seriousness and conviction that he or she *can* get better, the efforts *will* pay off, the games *must* end.

Can this make the schizophrenic violent?

Violence under any condition is absolutely unacceptable. Threats and intimidation must be confronted and corrected directly and clearly. Use a tough approach. Hospitalize if necessary. Real violence occurs only when the schizophrenic feels cornered or trapped in a hopeless situation. Keeping the schizophrenic busy with normal, useful activity is anything but hopeless. Talking seriously and firmly with the schizophrenic is a sign of caring, not a hostile rejection, and no matter how sick he or she is, the schizophrenic will understand the family's honest efforts. Recovering schizophrenics do want to activate themselves, to get well, to act and feel normal. When schizophrenics do not try, it is because they are stubbornly afraid to go ahead. At this phase of rehabilitation, the threat of violence has long disappeared and the core of hopelessness is replaced by the secret hope that the deadly seriousness of the family and counselor means there is an attainable, pleasant future ahead of the schizophrenic.

What does the family do when the schizophrenic does start working and attending social activities?

At this point the family's tensions are, of course, relieved because they can see the schizophrenic's progress. Whether or not they show it, the schizophrenics themselves are pleased as well to be active and useful, and glad to go on increasing the amount of activity for each day—eventually moving from five active days a week to seven. In even the more severe cases, and even when a family makes plenty of mistakes, schizophrenics can usually graduate to full active lives, if not yet to full-time employment, within six months.

What social activities should the schizophrenic participate in?

At Christmas the schizophrenic's social life should take the form of relaxed simplicity—going shopping, visiting with friends for brief periods of time, going to the movies with anyone with whom the schizophrenic feels comfortable. Social activities should be brief and easygoing at first, graduating to longer and more involved activities such as bowling, having friends visit, or going to a party. The best type of regular social contacts are those with other schizophrenics who are bound to be patient and understanding. Like shy teenagers, schizophrenics may balk at involving themselves in social activities for fear of embarrassing themselves, being "wallflowers," and because they are afraid to become activated.

As the schizophrenic gains confidence, the family should patiently but firmly help the patient renew his or her social life through low-key, pleasant activities such as going out to lunch with other schizophrenics, going to the movies, bowling, attending potluck suppers and beach parties, and visiting each other. Schizophrenics like to do all the things nonschizophrenics like to do.

In time, many schizophrenics come to "help themselves through helping others." For whatever reasons, visiting old people in nursing homes and participating in volunteer work of many kinds, especially that involving elderly people, seems to be very rewarding for schizophrenics.

Because many schizophrenics are self-conscious about their bodies, they are often reluctant at first to go swimming or to the beach. Almost invariably, the schizophrenic who hesitates to take part in one social activity is being controlled by a specific fear, such as self-consciousness about swimming, fear of clumsiness while bowling, fear of being ignored in a new social arena, fear that his or her cooked dish will not be acceptable at a potluck supper, and so on. Many of these fears can be talked out, faced, and resolved satisfactorily through simple understanding accompanied by a firm attitude from the family.

The family will see that as activities actually take place, the schizophrenic gradually gets involved with normal social events through the development of contacts with family friends, social and volunteer activities, and the worlds of work and school. As the schizophrenic improves, he or she will prefer more normal people, and it is important for the anxious family who wish to normalize their schizophrenic's social life not to hurry this process because it is a natural one that takes time.

Once the schizophrenic has become quite active, what is the next step?

Volunteer or part-time paid work usually is the next step, though much depends on the availability of suitable employment, which should be simple and unhurried at first. In rural areas general farm work is ideal, but in suburban areas it can be difficult to find the kind of simple, easygoing work the schizophrenic can do. In any case, the family and counselor must use their ingenuity in making use of whatever local volunteer and paid work is available. One of the problems of volunteer activities is that they tend to be scheduled only once or twice a week when the schizophrenic needs them every day. An hour or two of volunteer or paid work each day structures the schizophrenic's life much better and more simply than a whole day once a week. One of the most successful of these activities can be cafeteria work for daily senior citizens' lunches. City schizophrenics usually have access to some sort of organized day center or "club" that can offer not only daily activities but also a wide variety of employment information.

Why hasn't school been mentioned so far in schizophrenia rehabilitation?

School takes what schizophrenics don't have at first—concentration, organization, clear thinking, and initiative to study. Schizophrenics usually benefit most from starting with at-home activity, then proceeding to part-time volunteer work, then to part-time paid work, next to full-time work, and only *then* going back to school. Also, after working a while, many schizophrenics may choose very different and more appropriate schools than they would have if they returned to school before working, since their interests often crystallize during this period. Doing simple work is much easier than going to school and is nearly always best to start off with. Acute and milder schizophrenics, however, can and do return to school and do well.

What vocational problems will the schizophrenic have?

Aside from generally avoiding leadership and executive roles, schizophrenics really have no more vocational problems than nonschizophrenics. The vocational problems they do have invariably stem from relapses due to carelessness with the dos and don'ts. Unfortunately, even one relapse caused by the schizophrenic's cockiness, which causes him or her to ignore the dos and don'ts while working at a job, can seriously set the schizophrenic back vocationally because there may not be many jobs in the area. Otherwise, the process of vocational choice for an average schizophrenic is the same as for a nonschizophrenic. The most severely afflicted schizophrenics and multihandicapped schizophrenics, such as those with arthritis, mental retardation, or epileptic seizures, may find that occupation at a day care center or sheltered workshop is the best they can do for a considerable period of time, or permanently.

13

The schizophrenic, the family, and the counselor

What does the schizophrenia counselor do? Or what role does the schizophrenia counselor play?

The schizophrenia counselor works with the schizophrenic and family to promote every possible rehabilitation activity.

Sometimes the psychiatrist does this, but an increasing number of schizophrenics and families are counseled by other professionals—nurses, psychologists, or social workers. In part, this is a result of the fact that not enough psychiatrists are interested in schizophrenia; they also are usually expensive. In addition, the vast majority of the management problems of the schizophrenic and family are really rehabilitative problems rather than medical problems. Today trained schizophrenic rehabilitation counselors can do as well as or better than psychiatrists. Unhappily, there are few counselors who are well trained in any kind of rehabilitation at present, especially in the field of mental illness. Most modern schizophrenia counselors pick up their knowledge through experience, and, as a result, never really develop the kind of expertise they could get from thorough training. Even most psychiatrists are not trained in the educative and rehabilitation techniques so important to the treatment of schizophrenia.

What do schizophrenia counselors actually do?

They see the patient and family regularly to talk over every conceivable aspect of the practical problems that the schizophrenic and family have. They educate and encourage, help identify and solve problems, help schizophrenics find social activity and work in the community, suggest appropriate schools and living conditions, and so on. Counselors serve as a bridge for communication between the schizophrenic and family, friends, and other essential people in the community. Through individual personal counseling, they help the schizophrenic and various members of the family find confidence through understanding, knowledge, reassurance, and education about the schizophrenic's illness as well as about their own inner feelings. Counselors work with the schizophrenic and family to implement the dos and don'ts carefully and to maintain the rehabilitation momentum.

One of the major functions of the counselor is to help pace the enthusiasm that waxes and wanes during the rehabilitation period. Schizophrenics and families go through the same rehabilitation cycles as patients with other disorders. When their condition is clearly improving they are enthusiastic about their progress, but when things are not going well they feel discouraged and tend to slow down their efforts. Families of schizophrenics must instill some stability in the rehabilitation efforts; otherwise, the patients may relapse if the families let them get too stimulated during peaks of their progress or too discouraged when the inevitable defeats in rehabilitation come along. When they do well, schizophrenics often become overconfident and attempt to take on too much responsibility or too much work too soon. This can lead to a mini-relapse with its attendant discouragement and worry. The counselor and family must work together toward providing the most healthful environment for the schizophrenic—a quiet, easygoing, confidence-inspiring atmosphere that is relatively free from major ups and downs.

When usually conscientious schizophrenics start to act as if they just don't care anymore, what can the family and counselor do?

This naturally happens during rehabilitation of patients with any disorder. The family can try to understand the entire problem from the schizophrenic's point of view. Beginning rehabilitation is a big job that requires many major changes in the household. For instance, it can seem as if overnight the schizophrenic suddenly has to stop drinking; start taking medication regularly; start going to bed early; and give up coffee, tea, Coke, late parties, cakes, and cookies. As one author put it, it often seems as if the schizophrenic has to "give up everything that tastes good or is fun." In addition, the schizophrenic (and often the family, too) is resisting acceptance of the disorder itself and is likely to apply trial and error to the dos and don'ts to see whether or not violations will really bring on a relapse.

It is no wonder, then, that schizophrenics, like ordinary mortals, get tired of trying and feel overwhelmed by how much must be done. During the confusion of these important tasks they often lose perspective, finding it difficult to see any progress and sometimes reaching the point at which they just do not care. Clearly such low points are inevitable and normal while the schizophrenic and family are learning the hard way by experiencing both successes and failures. Here the counselor and family can use their greatest ingenuity to combine compassion and understanding with their loving toughness in order to keep the schizophrenic trying and to help him or her with discouragements, so that the patient does not lose the momentum of recovery.

Since the counselor does most of the rehabilitative work with the patient and family, what does the psychiatrist do?

Psychiatrists prescribe medications, monitor the patient's physical and mental health, and manage the schizophrenic and medications according to whatever other disorders he or she may have. They also continuously adjust medications to meet situations that crop up at home during the normal ups and downs of rehabilitation. It is important, however, that the psychiatrist and counselor be in close touch with each other. Medical management must be very closely coordinated with the rest of the treatment during the rehabilitation period. Good rehabilitation results in fairly rapid changes in both the physical and mental condition of the patient, so regular monitoring of medications is essential to avoid overmedication. These medication problems cannot be underestimated. For instance, one study showed that at least one-third of all the patients in several institutions were more crippled by side effects of medications than by their schizophrenia—clearly a horrible result of poor medical management! The counselor often will recommend adjustment in medications to the psychiatrist because he or she is most likely to know the family best.

Then the schizophrenic and family should see both the counselor and the psychiatrist?

Yes. At first, visits should be made to both—occasionally together in times of urgency—and often, usually at least once or twice a week until the rehabilitation is well under way. There is practically no such thing as a smooth, simple rehabilitation, so getting it off to a good start is essential.

Why is rehabilitation so complicated?

Families are not made up of mechanical robots—each member is a complicated person in his or her own right. Each family member has personality, individual needs and frailties, plus other illnesses. The idea that the schizophrenic is "sick" and that the family is "well" is only for beginners in the field. Experienced professional counselors know that *each family member has individual rights that are just as important as those of the schizophrenic.* They know that compromises, exceptions, complications, and negotiations are the rule as rehabilitation progresses. When there is only one family car, for instance, and Dad has to get to work, the schizophrenic has to get to a weekly group, and the brother has to get to the local college all in the same morning, there is clearly an important practical problem to be solved. No one of these three people is more or less important than the other, and satisfactory transportation has to be worked out for each one. Plenty of similar situations arise within each family during rehabilitation, and when mixed with such things as Mother's migraine headaches, wife's job pressures, brother's homework problems, or husband's golf game, engineering a successful rehabilitation can be a work of art, a proud skill.

Suppose something goes wrong at home? Won't the counselor be angry if someone calls?

Generally, counselors and doctors should have regular phone hours to help manage ordinary problems that arise in between interviews. One or the other should also be available to provide competent assistance in the case of emergencies such as drug reactions or whatever else worries the family. Arranging solid communications with the doctor and the counselor right at the beginning helps establish a good relationship between family and professionals and also ensures that all questions will be answered and all crises solved during the important and trying early stages of rehabilitation. These crisis problems often arise without warning, somehow *never* during the counselor's regular working hours! But it is interesting that professionals have discovered that when patients know they can call, they seldom seem to need to. Apparently, the family who isn't afraid to call the counselor during working hours usually can anticipate and/or prevent crises that could erupt into major episodes during nights, weekends, and holidays.

Does this imply that there is a technique for handling a counselor or doctor?

Precisely! Very often, patients and families put the counselor and doctor on some sort of pedestal, which suggests that the counselor is somehow above human status. Doctors and counselors are very human, indeed. They wouldn't be doing this type of work if they didn't need to be needed, just like the rest of us. So it is a mistake for the patient and family to think that the counselor handles the patient and family but that the family and patient shouldn't need to know how to handle the counselor. Doctors and counselors have the same feelings and needs that others have, and it is no secret that one of the basic satisfactions for counselors is being able to help the patient and family. Counselors thrive on appreciation and praise.

If the patient and family are appreciative of the counselor's efforts, are they likely to get better attention?

Right again! Most doctors and counselors are really trying to help. Showing appreciation of their genuine efforts sets up a good rapport among the patient, the family, and the counselor. As a result, the professionals may tend to go out of their way to be helpful. For the patient and family using insurance, Medicaid, or some other impersonal payment system, appreciation and praise are a kind of valued personal payment to the counselor for his or her efforts. The patient and family can also point out pleasant features of the counselor's personality and office as well. Simply put, it doesn't hurt to butter up the counselor a little bit here and there.

How does the family manage the counselor who seems to be missing a vital issue?

If the patient and family have been nurturing good relations with the counselor, the counselor is likely to be less defensive when the patient and family bring up criticisms such as the problems caused by excessive medications, medication side effects, or the counselor's lack of understanding on some point that the family feels strongly about. Under all circumstances, the patient and family must directly and candidly bring up practical problems they encounter so that they can be solved.

What should the family do if the counselor gets angry?

If the counselor overreacts or gets upset for some reason, the patient and family must understand that the counselor is human, too, and would not be so upset if he didn't care! A counselor who doesn't care will just ignore the whole problem, in which case the family should find a new counselor. The best way they can react is to reexamine the situation as thoroughly as possible and bring it up again later when the counselor is in a better mood. They should not just drop an important or controversial subject for fear of upsetting the counselor.

What happens if the schizophrenic and family just do not get along with the counselor or doctor?

When there is still constant tension between the counselor, the family, and the schizophrenic after an honest effort has been made to resolve it, the family and schizophrenic should look for another counselor to avoid sustaining a toxic situation.

How does the family find a good counselor?

This is done in the same way the family finds the best psychiatrist—by asking around. Other families that include a schizophrenic are the best single source of information, but schizophrenic specialists, local psychiatrists, or other professionals may be helpful as well. When dealing with a fairly large agency such as a community health center or family agency, try asking the secretary or counseling professional, "Which of the counselors, if any, would you ask to see *your* schizophrenic husband, wife, sister, or brother?" Many agencies assign counselors on a rotation basis so that the best counselors won't be all booked up and the least competent will have something to do, which makes for many difficult problems in getting the best counselors. Private counselors often are more capable than agency staff because they are good enough to attract patients on their own. However, in the field of schizophrenia, few private counselors have had the special rehabilitative training required for schizophrenia. In any community there is no substitute for obtaining several recommendations. When one counselor's name crops up from several different sources, she or he is probably good.

Regardless of how the family actually finds a good counselor, everyone must remember that no counselor is always right, no one is perfect, and that it is not the counselor's job to solve all problems, but to point out alternatives, help with communications, and suggest solutions. It is the patient's and family's job actually to provide solutions to the patient's problems. The good counselor should be a friend, advisor, confidante, and educator, but not a miracle worker.

Are there support groups for schizophrenics?

Yes. Call or write the National Alliance for the Mentally Ill. (See Bibliography for address and phone number) to locate the group in your area. If there isn't any, visit the closest one and start one in your area!

14

Stigma

How is the stigma problem of schizophrenia best handled?

In the long run, the best way to handle the stigma that surrounds schizophrenia is to make sure the patient gets well because in general people tend to treat others the way they act. The closer to normal the schizophrenic is, the more normal he or she appears. A second method is to prepare the schizophrenic to accept the occasional loss of an old friend who may need to stay away because the friend fears that the schizophrenia is somehow contagious. In practice, schizophrenics who make a solid recovery do not lose many friends. It is the patient's and family's fear of the stigma that usually does the most damage because it often leads them to hide or disguise the patient's disorder. This process of hiding invariably robs the patient of confidence and assertiveness through the guilt of having a mental illness.

Frankly facing the stigma of schizophrenia in the family through straightforward discussion—usually with a psychiatrist or counselor present—is an important part of every schizophrenic's recovery. Conversation is started simply by asking the schizophrenic if he or she is facing problems because he or she has been in a mental hospital or because people know about the schizophrenia. Some schizophrenics will meet with stigma problems and some will not. Those who do should then be asked what actually happened and what their reaction was. At that point, whatever problem arises can be handled by the family and counselor. This process can often be handled better in a group setting with other schizophrenics than within the family itself because of the understanding and support given by the other schizophrenics who have already resolved these problems. Stigma problems vary widely so that sometimes very little discussion is necessary. On the other hand, the problem may be quite significant so that a good deal of time may need to be spent supporting and reassuring the patient.

Suppose the schizophrenic doesn't seem interested in discussing the stigma?

The truth is that at first the schizophrenic is so much more involved in coping with the mental disorder, and with socializing with other patients and getting along with the family, that stigma problems are really not as important as the family may think. So, in the beginning, this discussion may seem irrelevant to the family and the schizophrenic may be noncommittal. It is usually later, when the schizophrenic graduates into normal society, that he or she encounters stigma reactions from children, neighbors, employers, friends, and the general public. At this time, the subject of stigma should be tactfully reintroduced. This also is best accomplished in a group setting because the group will include schizophrenics at different stages of recovery who can help each other accept their disorders from different perspectives. Patients who have already ventured forth into the world report to the group about their actual difficulties with stigma problems. Since these problems are usually relatively minor, such discussion will reassure the schizophrenic. If there is a major problem, family members can be invited to visit the group and join in this discussion.

What should schizophrenics do if they are laughed at, teased, or ignored because of their schizophrenia?

First, they must learn to accept their injured feelings just as every handicapped person does. At times life is difficult, and there is no real way to shield anybody, including the schizophrenic, from this fact. Second, the schizophrenic must learn to work at minimizing the handicap by learning to act and dress as normally as possible. The schizophrenic must learn whether the schizophrenic behavior provokes people's laughter or teasing. Unfortunately, he or she will often misinterpret the situation out of self-consciousness, mistakenly taking offense when none is intended. Frowzy makeup, sloppy or unusual clothes, and peculiar mannerisms, however, usually provoke the public into ridiculing the patient's behavior, whether or not it is fair or just. Wishing that people were different is hardly as useful as learning to act in a normal manner.

When a schizophrenic actually has been ridiculed, it can be helpful for the patient to compare his lot with that of patients who have other major disorders. In relation to paraplegics who must be confined in a wheelchair permanently or people who have multiple sclerosis and are always getting worse, the schizophrenic invariably seems much more fortunate. Constant resentful attitudes only result in a slowing down of rehabilitation, but positive attitudes increase the schizophrenic's energy and motivation toward recovery.

What should schizophrenics do on the spot when they are being ridiculed?

The only thing the schizophrenic can do is to sweat it out, "do as well as he can!"—after all, the patient can't just stay in the house all the time. In addition, the family can offer a hug and some encouragement when they see the schizophrenic's feelings are hurt or that he or she is reluctant to try again.

This "cosmetic" aspect of the schizophrenic's behavior—the facial expressions and manner that reveal the schizophrenia to the public—must be discussed and corrected to help the schizophrenic appear more normal. Fortunately, most of these cosmetic problems gradually diminish or totally disappear as the rehabilitation proceeds. It is pleasant indeed, for instance, to watch the recovering schizophrenic woman begin to realize that she is being stared at because she is attractive rather than because she is schizophrenic!

How does the schizophrenic handle injured feelings?

The best way to handle all feelings—and hurt feelings especially—is to talk about them with other schizophrenics, the psychiatrist, the counselor, and the family. The outpatient discussion group for schizophrenics is absolutely invaluable to the management of hurt feelings because issues of stigma, socialization, denial, and acceptance are much easier to handle when the schizophrenics learn they are not alone in these experiences. Thus they learn from one another and from the group leader about what they can do to prevent these problems. They learn that the best attack on stigma is normal involvement in active living—not in isolation. Social activities, volunteer work, parties, and careers all gradually remove the "cosmetic" problems and develop the confidence required to abolish the stigma.

How does the family handle *its* stigma problems?

This is an important matter. The worst thing for the family to do is to continue to cover up. In fact, the family may be more biased and prejudiced against schizophrenia than the patient and friends are, causing them to hide their secret, cover up and lie about it, and so on. If this is a problem, it must be talked about and resolved with the counselor because the tangled web of deceit can easily involve the schizophrenic, who is already guilty and confused with having to handle the family's embarrassment too. On the other side of this coin, some well-meaning, psychologically-oriented families should be cautioned against making too much of stigma problems by talking about them more than necessary. It is just as harmful to the handicapped person to constantly draw attention to the handicap rather than to attaining normal living. In addition, talking a great deal about schizophrenia only rekindles the old painful emotional fears and memories that are not only hard to handle in themselves but have no constructive value.

How does stigma affect schizophrenics after they have recovered?

While they don't actually forget, the fact is that friends and neighbors have a way of ignoring a person's "nervous breakdown" after that person has returned to normal behavior. In their own minds, these people think of the formerly handicapped person as somehow different from all those "mentally ill types" that they have read about who are *really* crazy. That is, because this schizophrenic doesn't act like their preconceived image of "crazy," they feel that he really isn't schizophrenic. So when talking about the now recovered schizophrenic, most people tend to say, "Oh, yes, he had a little breakdown years ago, but he got over it." For this reason, it is extremely helpful for the recovering schizophrenic to meet fully recovered schizophrenics on a regular basis. These contacts have a reassuring effect on the schizophrenic's hope and motivation in the rehabilitation efforts. Meticulous attention to the schizophrenia itself through the dos and don'ts during the rehabilitation process is nonetheless the key to almost all the schizophrenic's stigma problems—in social life, work success, and personal confidence.

15

Driving the car and sexual matters

Can schizophrenics drive a car?

Absolutely! There is, in fact, some indication that even when they are taking antipsychotic medications schizophrenics actually have *fewer* auto accidents than nonschizophrenics. Naturally, no one should drive when his or her full attention is not on driving. But, after a few months, even with quite a severe illness, most schizophrenics can handle a car perfectly and drive safely with good judgment. In one study, out of thirty driving schizophrenics only three accidents—and no injuries—happened over a period of several years. Two of these accidents could be attributed to other causes: One of the drivers was an alcoholic, drug-addicted schizophrenic who was actively drinking; the other was a middle-aged woman who was later found out to have a separate brain disorder.

If there is doubt about the schizophrenic's ability to drive, a good way to clear up the matter is to arrange a driving test at any driving school. Common sense suggests that if the schizophrenic is still erratic about taking medications or still does not adhere to the dos and don'ts steadily, that person should not drive. When overmedicated or when having side effects from medications, schizophrenics should not drive because they cannot pay proper attention to the task. There is no reason why a stable schizophrenic should not drive tractors or trucks, or work around machinery.

Do schizophrenics have special problems with sex?

As with other illnesses, schizophrenics often have somewhat lower sexual urges, depending on the severity of the illness and how far the patient has proceeded in rehabilitation. However, this is by no means always true. Some antischizophrenic medications cause male schizophrenics to have difficulty in ejaculation or in attaining an erection. If this occurs, it should be discussed immediately with the psychiatrist because adjustments in medication are all that is needed.

Schizophrenia itself does not cause other sexual problems. After a reasonable period of rehabilitation, female schizophrenics tend to enjoy sex without difficulty, though, like men, they may have extra difficulty in reaching orgasm until their recovery is more complete. Schizophrenics seem to be unusually shy about bringing up sexual problems such as this and it is helpful for the family or counselor to bring up the matter with the schizophrenic once in a while if it seems necessary. Usually a frank discussion with an understanding schizophrenia specialist (about medications) and/or the counselor is really all that is necessary to clear up these problems satisfactorily. There is no reason why a schizophrenic should not read sex manuals or discuss sex exactly as everyone else does. Discussions of sex usually are better held in a one-to-one counseling situation than in a group or family setting.

What about homosexual schizophrenics?

Homosexuality probably occurs in schizophrenics about as often as it does in nonschizophrenics. It can be a difficult problem because there is a double stigma, so to speak, which only further aggravates the schizophrenia stigma. When the homosexual schizophrenic is well enough, he or she will probably benefit from seeing a homosexual counselor from a local gay organization. In actual life, most homosexual schizophrenics seem to resolve their "problem" simply by suppressing their sexuality or by masturbating so that the homosexuality does not surface among family and friends. However, homosexuality is a major issue for every schizophrenic and should be talked about and resolved in an understanding atmosphere.

Do schizophrenics have sexual deviations, too?

Certainly, but not in the large amounts that some popular stereotypes might suggest. Sexual deviations are such things as exhibitionism (showing genitals in public), sadomasochism (enjoying hurting or being hurt), fetishism (being aroused by objects such as women's clothes or rubber garments), and transvestism (men wearing women's clothes). What may appear as sexual deviations in the actively ill schizophrenic simply are the results of the same distortion that schizophrenia causes in every other kind of thought or action.

While most sexual deviations are actually only minor problems of daily living, they are always significant—even devastating—to the victim. Therefore, they should be faced firmly and frankly at an appropriate time with the counselor. The family must be ready to provide firm encouragement in case the schizophrenic is too embarrassed to talk about it. Clearly, this kind of topic should be broached only after a good relationship has been formed between the schizophrenic and the counselor.

Under all circumstances, sexual deviations remain unacceptable in our society and must not be revealed to the public by the schizophrenic or family. Exposing a patient's sexual problems may actually hinder the rehabilitation effort because schizophrenics simply do not have sufficient defense mechanisms to deal successfully with any amount of public condemnation or scorn. Although it may seem harsh to advocate this type of secrecy, I believe it is the only realistic approach. In fact, the counselor's tack usually is based on simply telling the schizophrenic not to expose himself, steal the clothes off the clothesline, or fondle children—all suppressive measures. This, too, may seem like harsh treatment, but I have observed in my counseling that straight suppressive commands, aphorisms, or flat statements seem to work best.

16

Economics of schizophrenia

Schizophrenia is an expensive long-term disorder. How do families manage these additional burdens?

In any major illness, the worse disaster occurs when the family breadwinner—husband, wife, mother, father—comes down with schizophrenia. If the schizophrenia lasts more than a few weeks, the use of savings, unemployment insurance, and mortgage borrowing may be necessary until he or she can return to work. In very severe cases some sort of Social Security disability pension may be needed. Fortunately, breadwinners usually are older and already have vocational skills so that when they come down with schizophrenia they almost always will return to work afterward—usually to the same job.

What kind of financial arrangements are made when the schizophrenic is not the breadwinner?

If the schizophrenic works, the family usually can struggle along with less income. If the schizophrenic is a mother with children, temporary alternate care for the children—through the family, neighbors, or through a community agency—may be sought while the patient is actively ill. Schizophrenic mothers also almost always get well enough to return to care for the children. If the schizophrenic is other than the breadwinner or mother, then the major problem lies in the expense of the treatment.

Does medical insurance such as Blue Cross cover schizophrenia?

At best, all schizophrenics undergo expensive treatment. Most insurance companies now provide at least $500 per patient per year for psychiatrists and counselors and about ninety days or more in the hospital for mental illness. This is a lot but is usually nowhere near enough to pay the counselor and/or psychiatrist for that first year due to the requirements of intense, early rehabilitation effort. Types of insurance usually cover the vast majority of the necessary hospital time for most schizophrenics. Most families will need to draw from savings or borrow money during this time.

Are there other sources of money to pay for schizophrenia?

In recent years schizophrenia has come to qualify as a disability disorder at state and federal Departments of Vocational Rehabilitation. These departments occasionally will fund psychiatric rehabilitative treatment for the schizophrenic. (Their phone numbers are listed under the specific state government in the phone book.) Unhappily, the state

Departments of Vocational Rehabilitation generally require considerable evaluation and paperwork in order to fund the rehabilitative work necessary—often taking from two to six months to complete. By this time, of course, the needs of the schizophrenic may have totally changed.

There is a Federal Social Security Disability System (which can be located in the phone book under United States Government) for which an application can be made if certain requirements are met. These disabilities usually pay most medical expenses and also provide a monthly living expense for the schizophrenic who qualifies. Other rehabilitation funding may be available from the Veterans Services, CHAMPUS, or CHAMP VA, depending on the relationship of the schizophrenic to the veteran involved. These can be located by calling any local veterans' organization or a veterans' representative under either state or federal phone book listings. Recreational, vocational, day-care centers, community residences, and other rehabilitative activity may also be provided under a private or government grant or funding of some type. Schizophrenics and families should waste no time in looking into these payment systems because payments are very often made retroactive to the date of application and they often take weeks or months to be processed.

In addition, it is simply a fact that many schizophrenics and their families do not learn of the wide variety of programs and activities available to them in their own communities. For instance, in some instances, disability grants are available to provide live-in companions for certain multihandicapped people. Schizophrenics can often get free nighttime or college courses. Sometimes free transportation, free meals, and food stamps can be obtained. Generally, local social workers who deal with schizophrenia are the best sources for this type of economic information and they should be consulted as soon as possible in the course of the schizophrenia.

What should families with limited finances think about first?

The place for the family to put whatever money it does have is into the early evaluation and diagnosis by the schizophrenia specialist. In this way, huge costs resulting from errors in diagnosis and treatment can be avoided. Before they settle for less than best, families should look for the best local rehabilitation system regardless of the cost, because quite often an unexpected method of payment may arise.

If patients receive disability pensions, won't that prevent them from working?

Unhappily, many government disability pensions have been unable to adapt to the requirements of many disorders, including schizophrenia. In general, whatever the disorder, pensions are based on full-time rather than on part-time work so that the amputee, the arthritic, and the schizophrenic who usually need to return gradually to full-time work cannot count on an adequate steady income throughout the rehabilitation period. These pensions, established under present laws, cannot adjust to the various in-between needs over the several months to two or three years required to attain a full-time paid position. The patient and family usually will need to provide some extra subsidy to the government pensions during this rehabilitative process.

In reality, social workers at these various departments are quite impressed by the conscientious efforts of a schizophrenic to return to full-time work, and they usually try to be as helpful as they can within the guidelines under which they must work. It is best to be truthful to these workers because in the long run the schizophrenic and family will obtain more practical financial help by doing so.

Is it true that people who try to return to work lose their pensions?

On the basis that the schizophrenic who works full-time no

longer requires a pension, the answer is no. Most pensions do allow for some kinds of rehabilitation efforts; patients and families should learn about these in detail from the appropriate sources because they vary a great deal from state to state and from situation to situation. When the schizophrenic does get a good job, he or she may lose the pension but usually can reapply for it if a relapse occurs. Some disability pensions allow for a period of time to be sure the handicapped person will be successful in the full-time job before the pension is dropped. This is extremely difficult for most people to understand because there are so many different types of pension plans and because the laws are so complicated. Sometimes a community advocate is provided by one of the local human services agencies who can help the schizophrenic and family to plow their way through the horrendous governmental red tape and confusion.

What else should a family look out for?

Disability pensions *can* be a psychological trap for patients when the disability is applied for too early. The temptation by the schizophrenic and family to sacrifice uncertain potential income for a present steady pension often requires the patient and family to spend a great deal of time and effort proving how sick the schizophrenic is rather than putting their attention into rehabilitation. Although the same temptation exists for other disorders, the ever-present myths about the dismal future in schizophrenia often prompts patients and families to act too quickly to obtain these pensions, thus sacrificing a productive financial future for the schizophrenic. In some instances, in fact, the guilty schizophrenic and family may feel unconsciously or semiconsciously required to prove to themselves continuously that the schizophrenic is really ill, thus doing great harm to the schizophrenic's future.

Review

The ten commandments for management of schizophrenia

In my office I have a mimeographed list that is given to patients even before I have formally labeled them "schizophrenic." The list is simply labeled "Dos and Don'ts" and is provided on the patient's first visit. The following is a similar version of the list.

1. Get at least eight hours' sleep every night.
2. Totally avoid stimulants—caffeine, diet pills, nasal decongestants, etc.
3. Do not drink alcoholic beverages or take other narcotics or sedatives.
4. Don't use any street drugs—marijuana, LSD, etc.
5. Eat minimum quantities of foods containing sugar, milk, corn, or wheat.
6. With your doctor's OK, gradually learn to jog twenty minutes a day without stopping.
7. Don't live in a toxic atmosphere.
8. Love more than one—don't put all your emotional eggs in one basket.
9. Take your medications at the same time and in the same amount every day.
10. Don't live alone.

Bibliography

I have tried to make the following bibliography as useful as possible for not only the general reader, but also I have included a basic scientific bibliography for those serious students of schizophrenia.

To locate one of the books, try your library first. Then the NAMI at 1234 Massachusetts Avenue, Northwest, Washinton, D.C. 2005. If no luck, go to a *small* bookstore and ask them to order it for you. Don't let them tell you the books mentioned here are "out of print." I urge you to donate these and other books to your library when you are through with them, so that the next schizophrenic or family member may find it there.

GENERAL

Bernheim, Kayla F., and Richard R. J. Lewine. *Schizophrenia: Symptoms, Causes and Treatments.* Paperback, W. W. Norton, 1979.

Bernheim, Kayla F., Richard R. J. Lewine, and Caroline T. Beale. *The Caring Family: Living with Chronic Mental Illness.* Cloth, Random House, 1980; paperback, Contemporary Books, 1984.

Kanter, Joel. *Coping Strategies for Relatives of the Mentally Ill.* Paperback, 1982. Order from the NAMI.

Snyder, Solomon H., M.D. *Biological Aspects of Mental Disorder.* Oxford University Press, 1980. Straightforward account of major developments in neurochemistry and genetics of mental disorder.

Torrey, E. Fuller. *Surviving Schizophrenia.* Harper & Row, 1983. A very helpful family manual.

Vine, Phyllis. *Families in Pain: Children, Siblings, Spouses, and Parents Speak Out.* Pantheon Press, 1982.

Wasow, Mona. *Coping with Schizophrenia: A Survival Manual for Parents, Relatives and Friends.* Paperback, Science and Behavior Books, 1982.

GENETIC DATA

Kendler, Kenneth, and C. Dennis Robinette. "Schizophrenia in the Academy of Sciences National Research Council Twin Registry: A 16-Year Update." *American Journal of Psychiatry,* vol. 140, no. 12. One of the two most recent key research reports.

Kety, Seymour S. "Mental Illness in the Biological and Adoptive Relatives of Schizophrenic Adoptees: Findings Relevant to Genetic and Environmental Factors in Etiology." *American Journal of Psychiatry,* vol. 140, no. 6, June 1983, pp. 720–27. One of the two most recent key research reports.

BRAIN SIZE IN SCHIZOPHRENIA

Weinberger, Daniel, M.D., and R. J. Wyatt. "Enlarged Cerebral Ventricles in Schizophrenia." *Psychiatric Annals,* 13:15, May 1983, p. 412. A good summary article on anatomical changes in schizophrenia from the NIMH.

BRAIN BIOCHEMISTRY

Snyder, Solomon H., M.D. "Dopamine Receptors, Neuroleptics and

Schizophrenia." *American Journal of Psychiatry,* vol. 138, no. 4, April 1981, pp. 460-64. Good summary and references for the scientist.

CAFFEINE

de Freitas, Brian, and George Schwartz. "Effects of Caffeine in Chronic Psychiatric Patient." *American Journal of Psychiatry,* vol. 136, no. 70, October 1979. Shows improvement in patients who had reduced caffeine intake.

Greeden, John F., et al. "Anxiety and Depression Associated with Caffeinism among Psychiatric Patients." *American Journal of Psychiatry,* vol. 135, no. 8, pp. 963-66, August 1978.

Mikkalsen, Edward J., M.D. "Caffeine and Schizophrenia." *Journal of Clinical Psychiatry,* 39:723, 736, September.

Winstead, Daniel K., M.D. "Coffee Consumption among Psychiatric Inpatients." *American Journal of Psychiatry,* vol. 133, no. 12, December 1976. Higher users have higher incidence of psychosis and longer hospital stays and more often use psychotropics.

PHYSIOLOGICAL DIFFERENCES BETWEEN SCHIZOPHRENICS AND NON-SCHIZOPHRENICS

Latham, C., and P. S. Holzman. "Optokinetic Nystagmus of Pursuit Eye Movements in Schizophrenics." *Archives of General Psychiatry,* vol, 38, no. 9, p. 997, September 1981. A sample of hundreds of researches showing schizophrenia affects the entire body.

NUTRITIONAL RESEARCH

Dohan, F. C., M.D., and J. C. Grasberger, M.D. "Relapsed Schizophrenics—Earlier Discharge from the Hospital after Cereal-Free and Milk-Free Diet." *American Journal of Psychiatry,* vol. 130, no. 6, June 1973. The first blockbuster report that diet affects schizophrenia.

Porter, J. M., and J. A. Horne. "Bedtime Food Supplements and Sleep: Effects of Different Carbohydrate Levels." Illustrates the type of research needed in schizophrenia. Good bibliography.

Singh, Wan Monan, and Stanley R. Kay. "Wheat Gluten as a Pathologic Factor in Schizophrenia." *Science,* vol. 19, January 1976, p. 401. This validates Dr. Dohan's research.

EXERCISE

"Antidepressant Running." *Psychiatric Annals,* 9(3):134:40, 1979. Validates the importance of running for depression.

Conroy, Robert W., M.D., et al. "Total Fitness as a Psychiatric Hospital Program." *Bulletin Meninger Clinic,* 45(1), 1981, pp. 65–71. Eighty-five percent showed some form of positive effects from intense daily exercise.

FAMILY TREATMENT

Anderson, Carl, Gerard E. Hogarty, and Douglas J. Reiss. "Family Treatment of Adult Schizophrenia Patients: A Psycho-Educational Approach." *Schizophrenia Bulletin,* vol. 6, no. 3, 1980. A good summary.

REHABILITATION IN SCHIZOPHRENIA

Mosher, Loren D., M.D., and Sam S. Keith, M.D. "Research on the Psychosocial Treatment of Schizophrenia: A Summary Report." *American Journal of Psychiatry,* vol 136, no. 5, May 1979, p. 623. Dr. Mosher says, "We know more about the diagnosis, treatment, and rehabilitation of schizophrenia than is generally acknowledged." An excellent summary on rehabilitation in schizophrenia by a very experienced group.

EFFECTIVENESS OF TREATMENT

Manschreck, Theo C. "Curent Concepts in Psychiatry: Schizophrenic Disorders." *New England Journal of Medicine,* vol. 305, no. 27, p. 1628, December 31, 1981. The best single up-to-date scientific article on schizophrenia.

May, Phillip R., M.D., et al. "Schizophrenia: A Follow-up Study of the Results of Five Forms of Treatment." *Archives of General Psychiatry,* vol. 38, July 1981, p. 776. Compares five groups of schizophrenics: (1) medications, (2) psychotherapy, (3) medications and psychotherapy, (4) electroconvulsive therapy (ECT), and (5) milieu treatment. ECT, meds worked best, psychotherapy worst.

Index